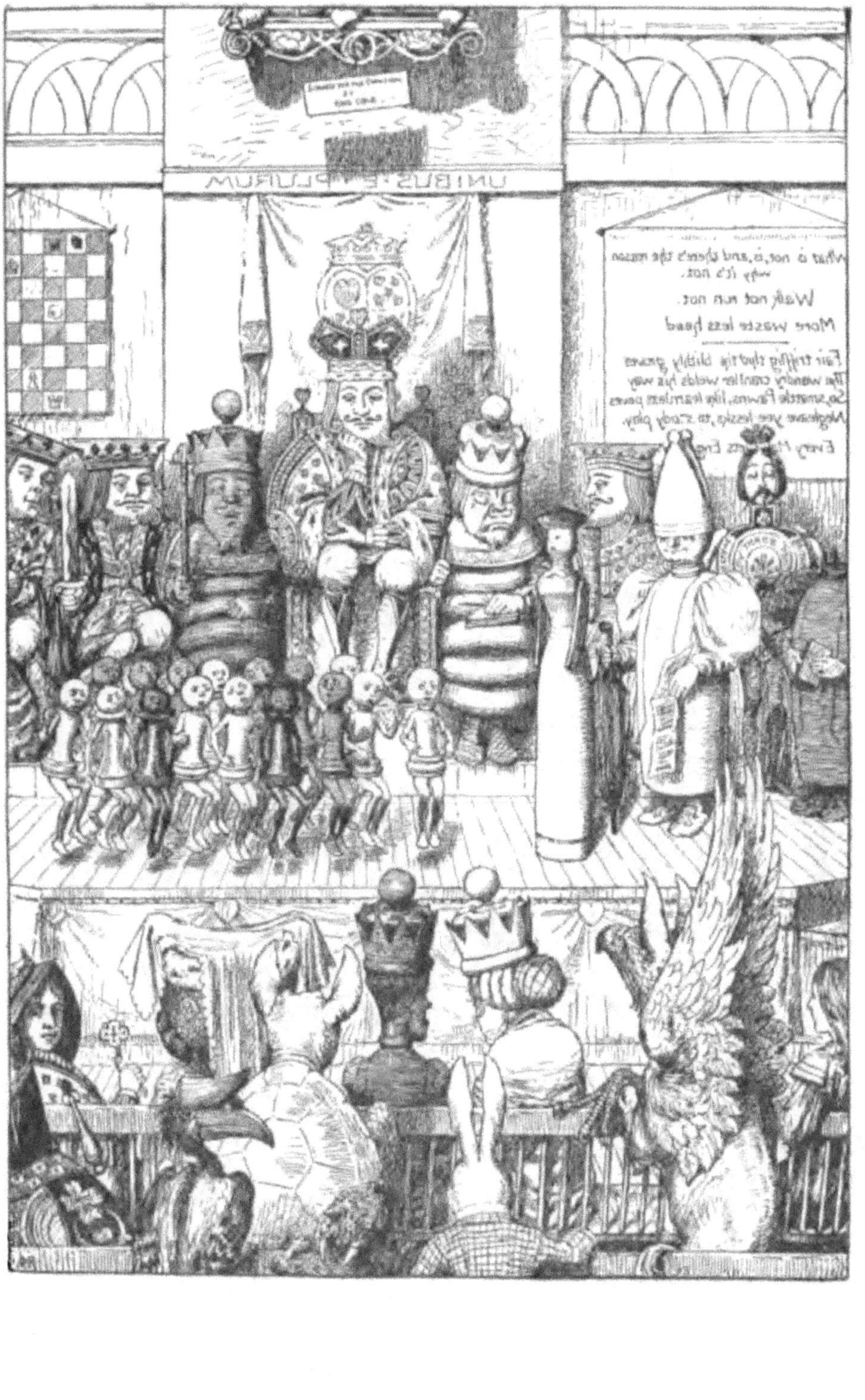

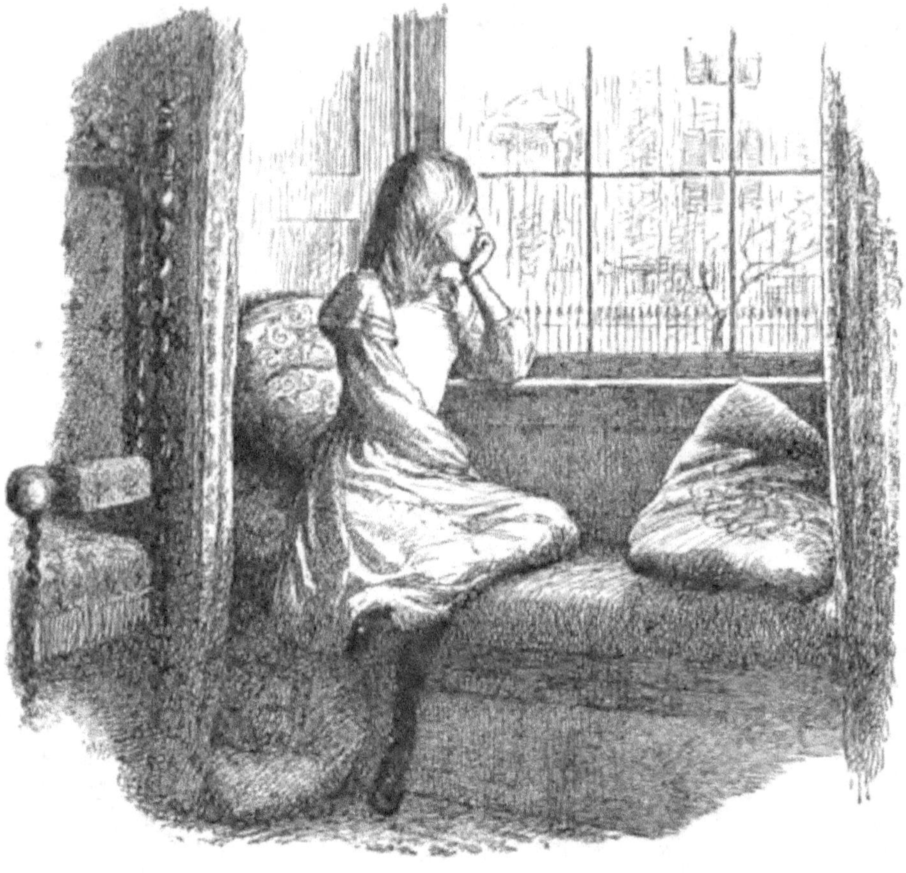

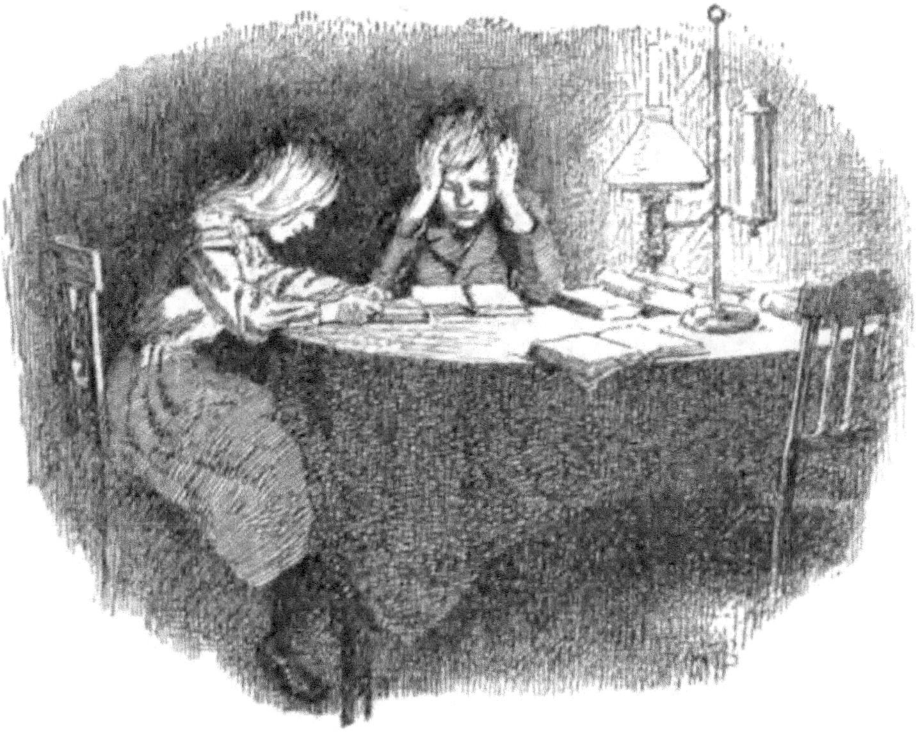

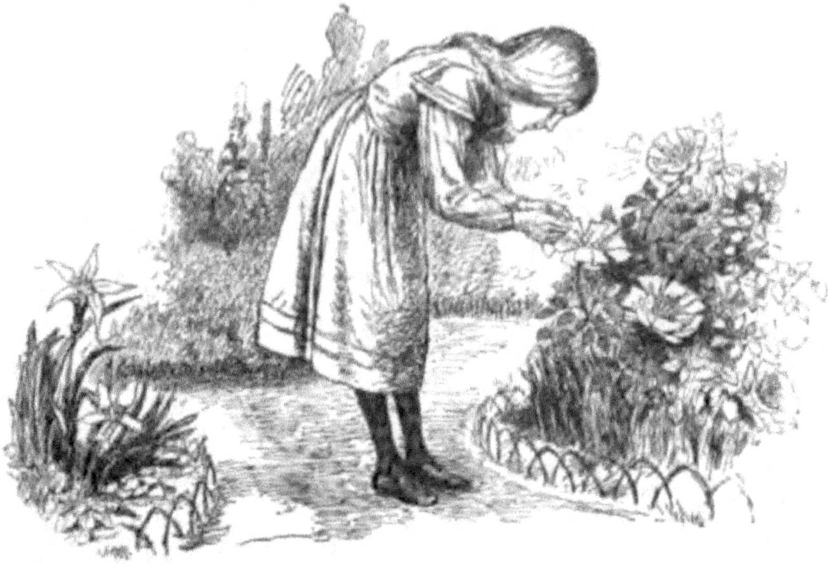

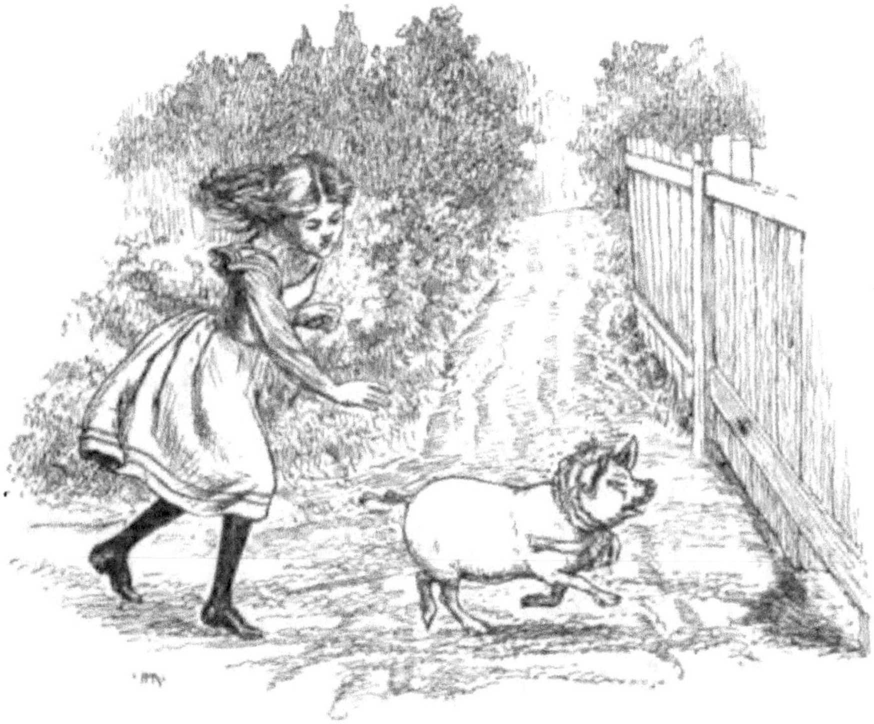

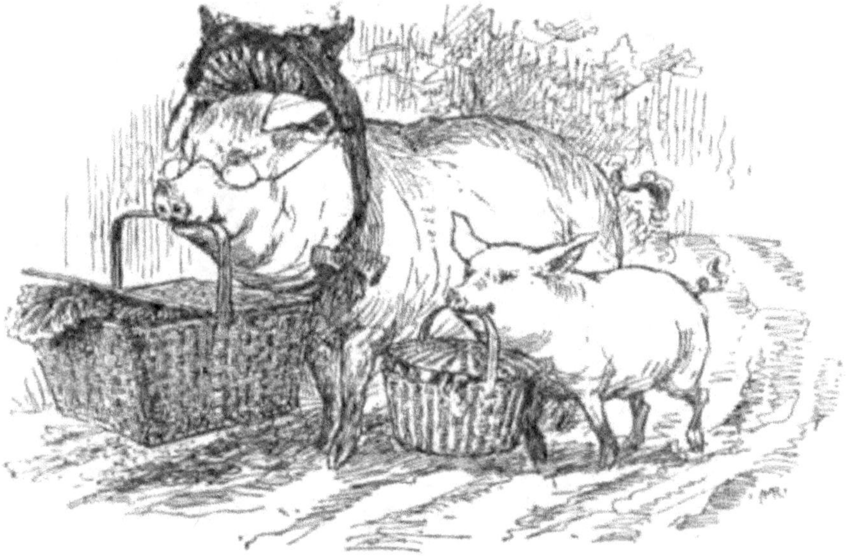

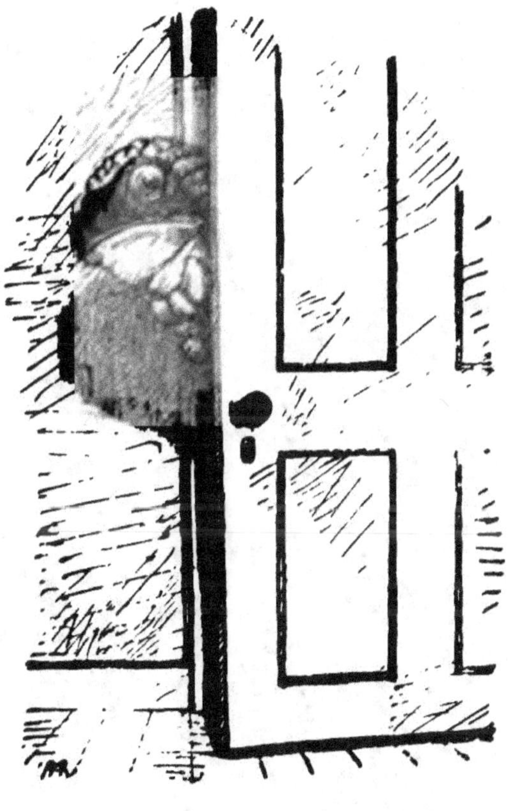

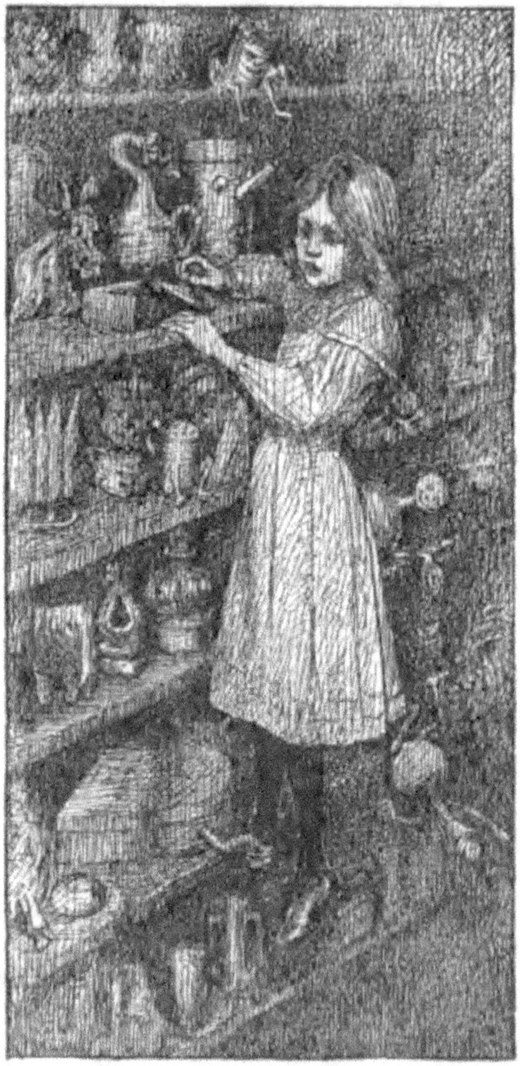

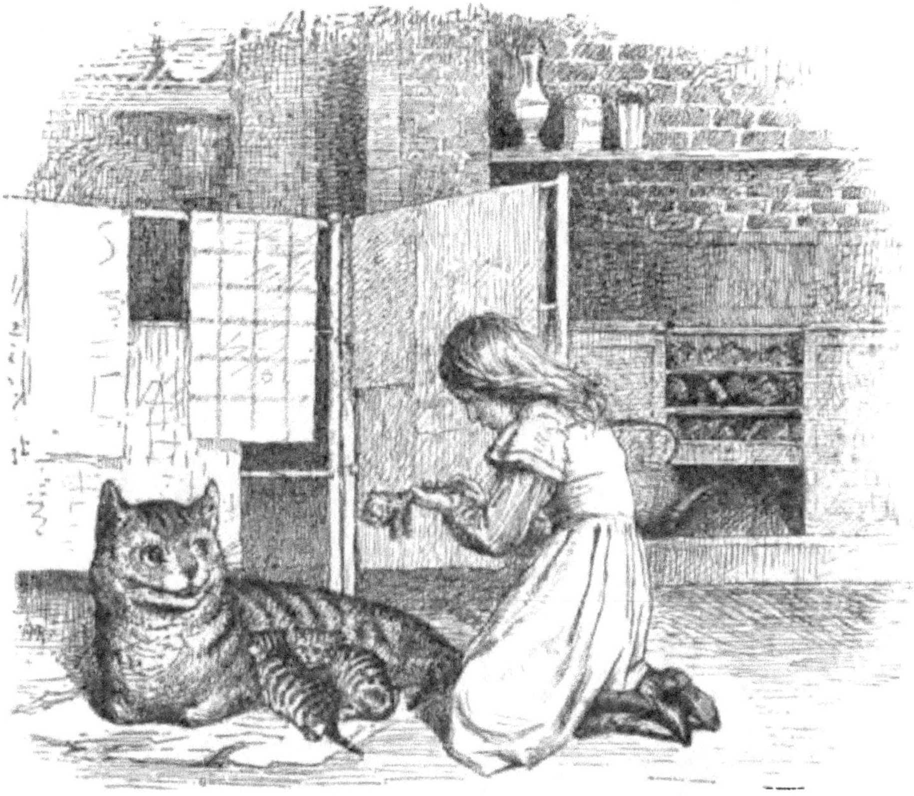

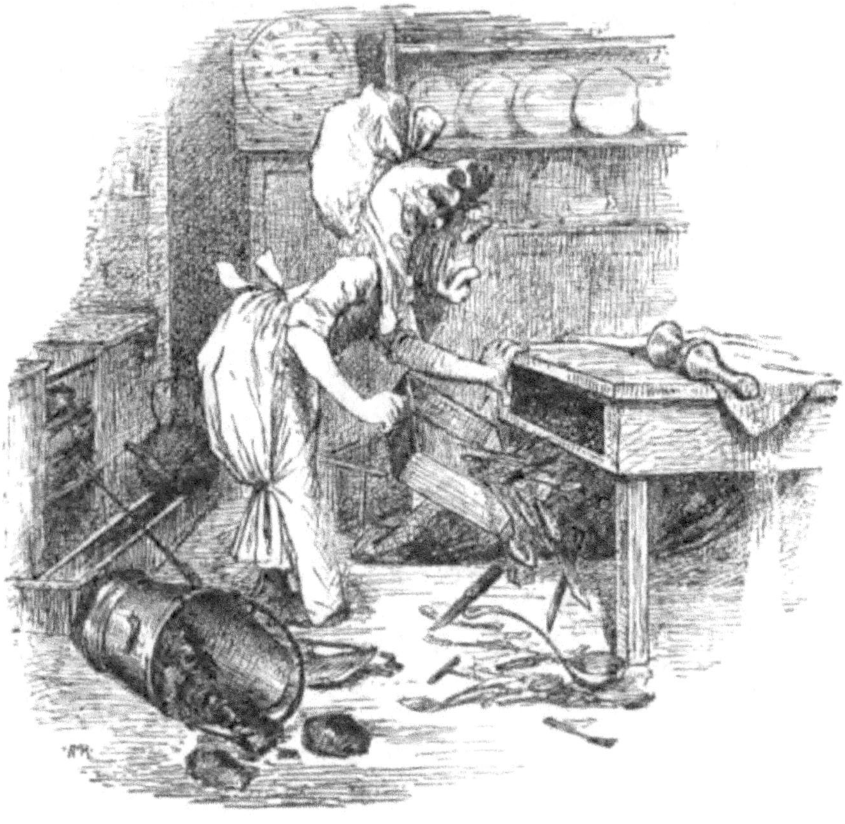

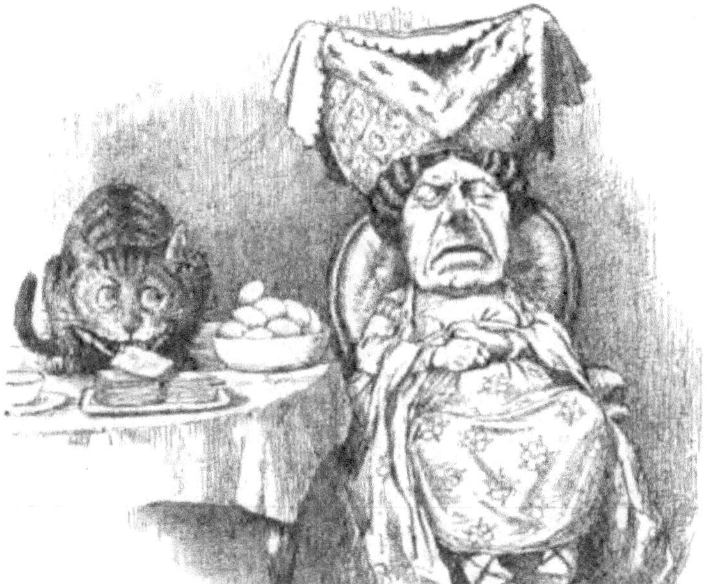

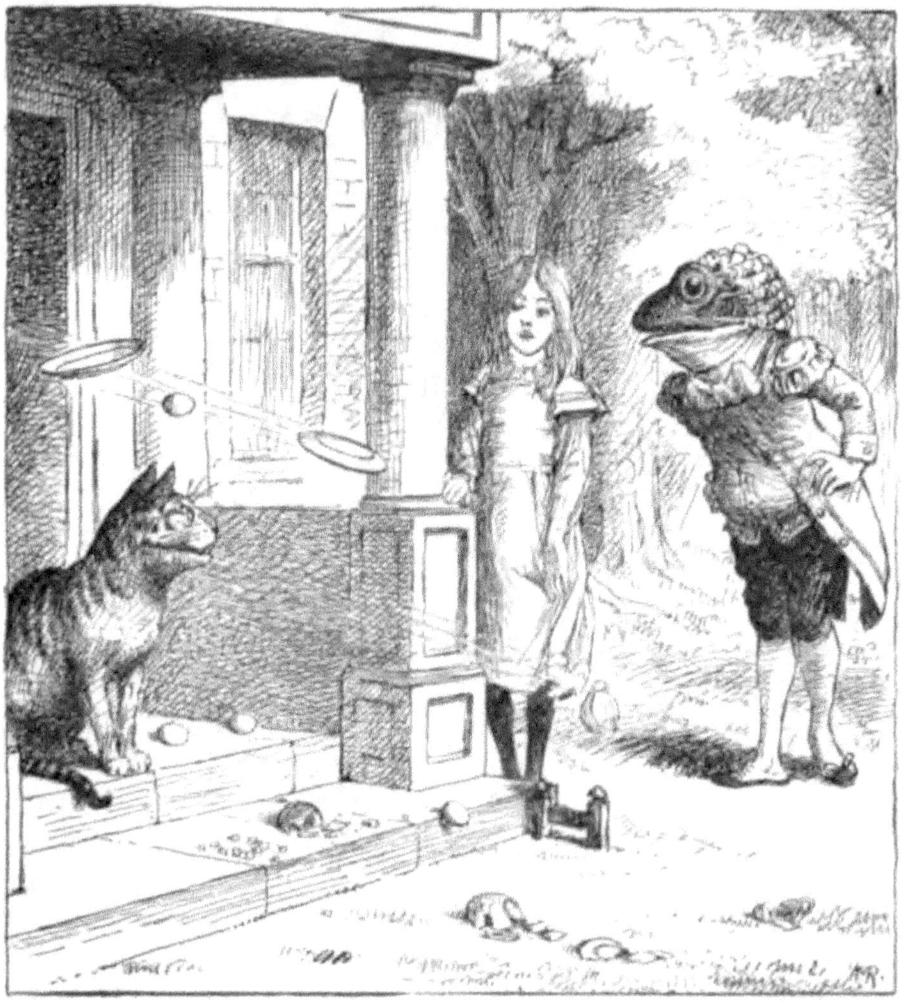

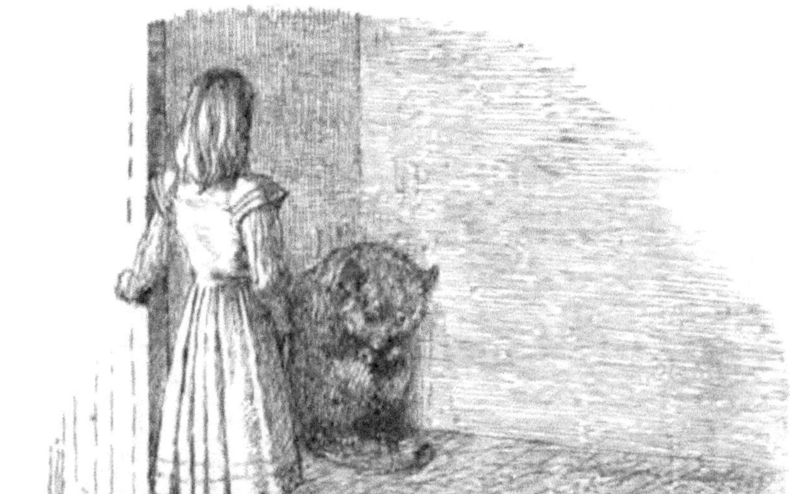

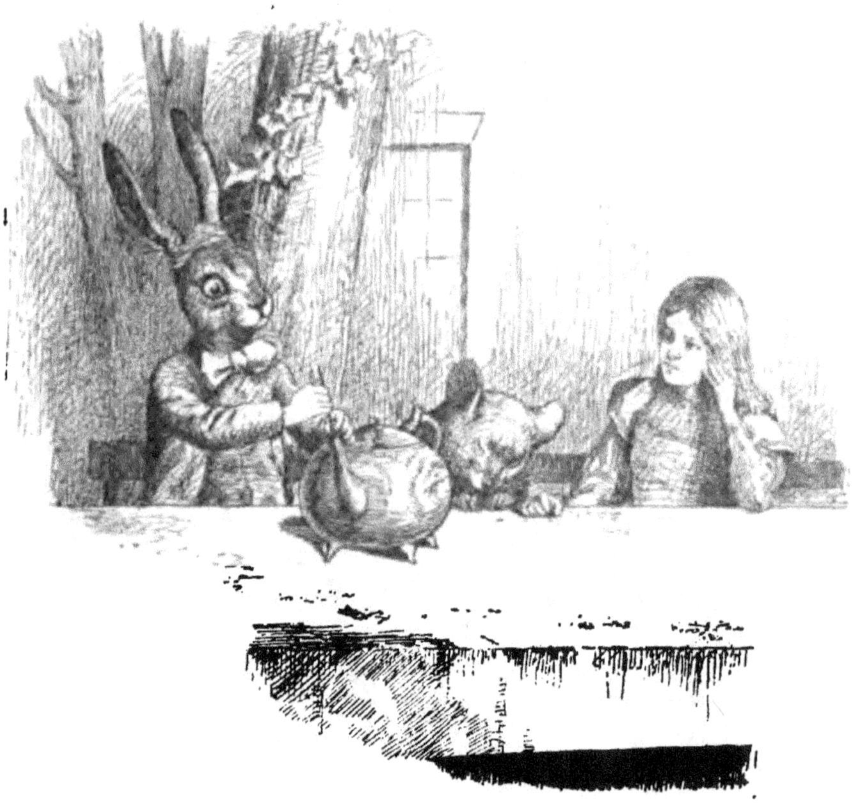

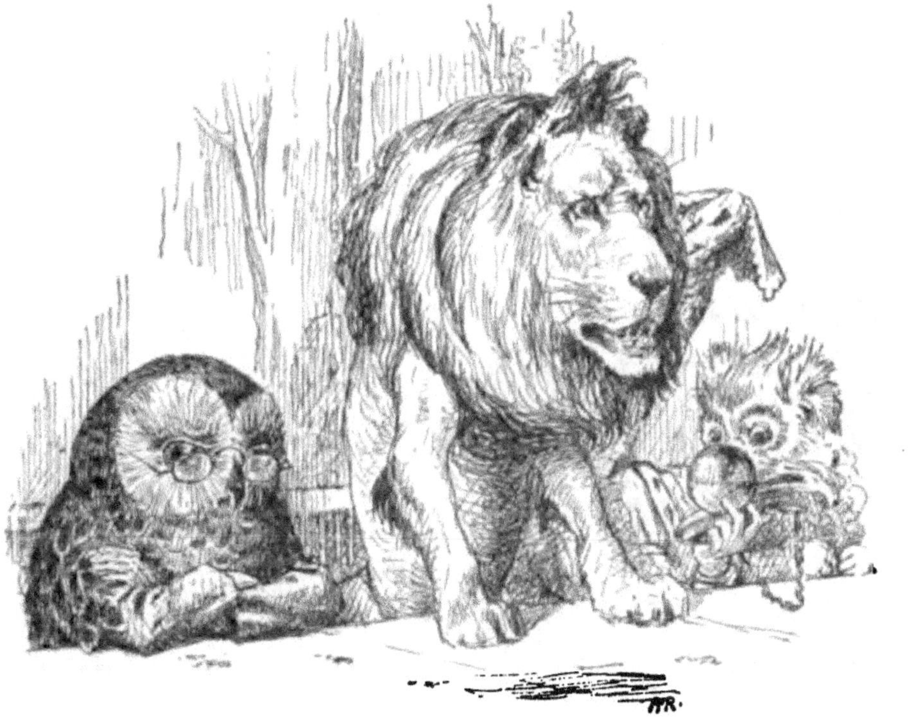

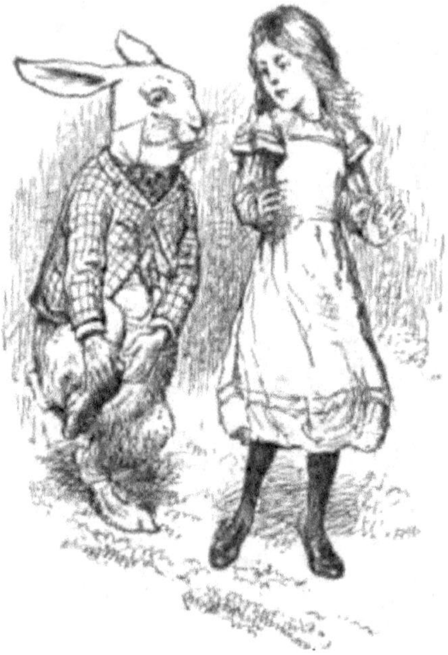

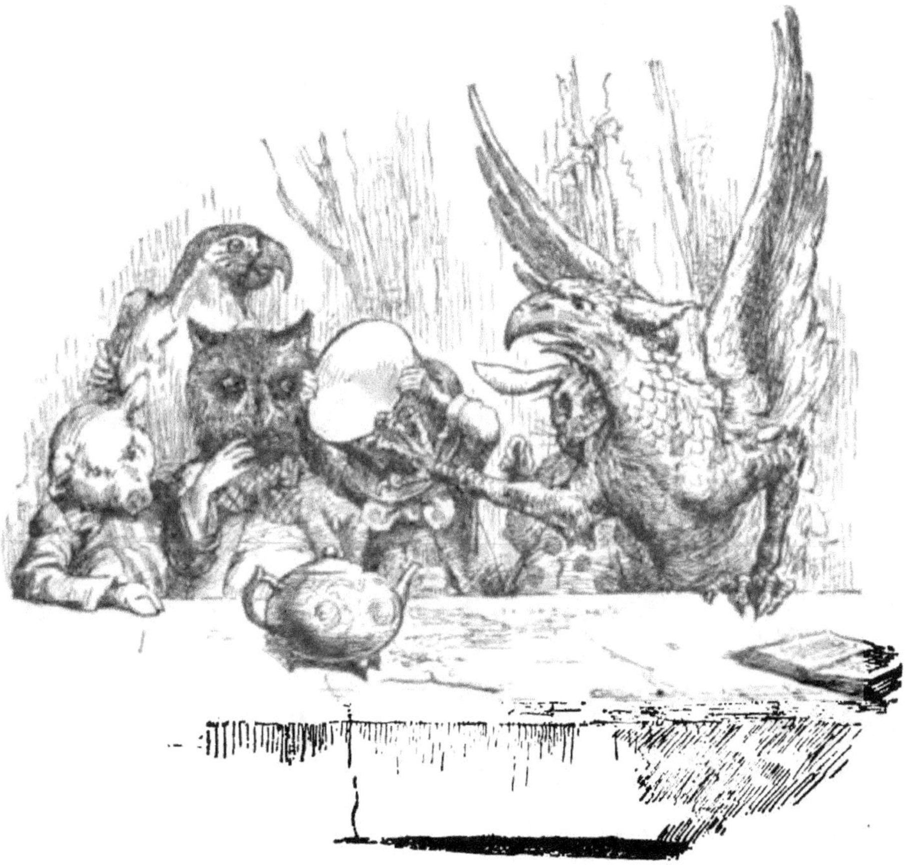

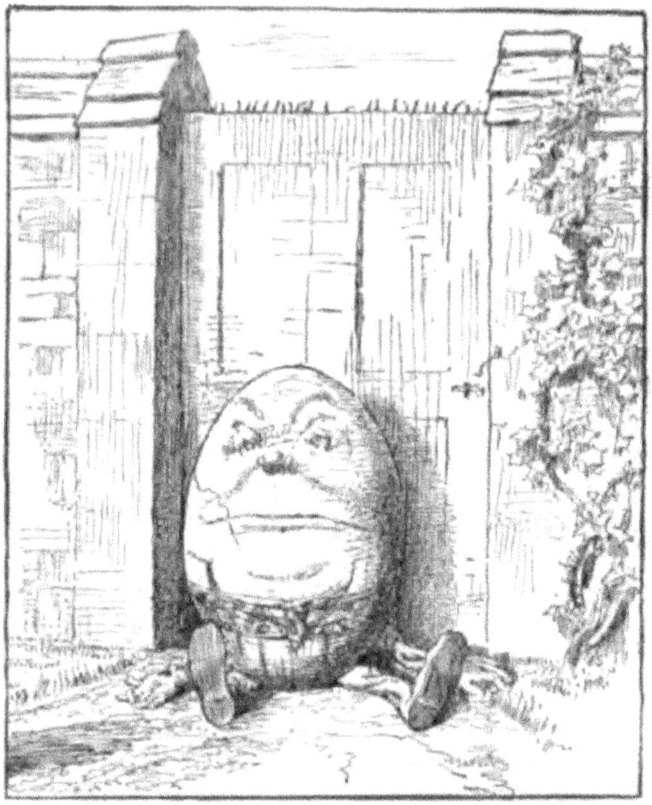

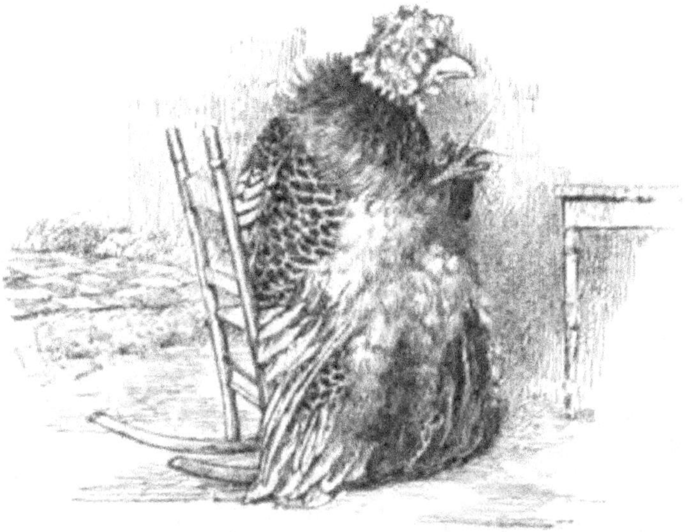

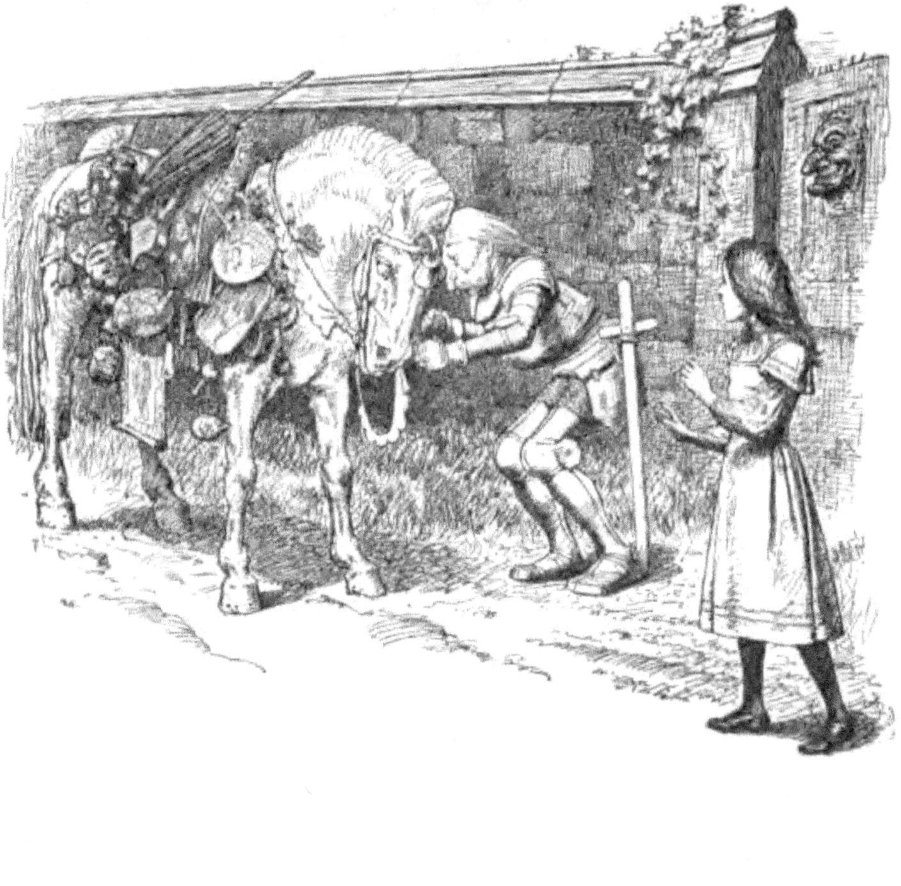

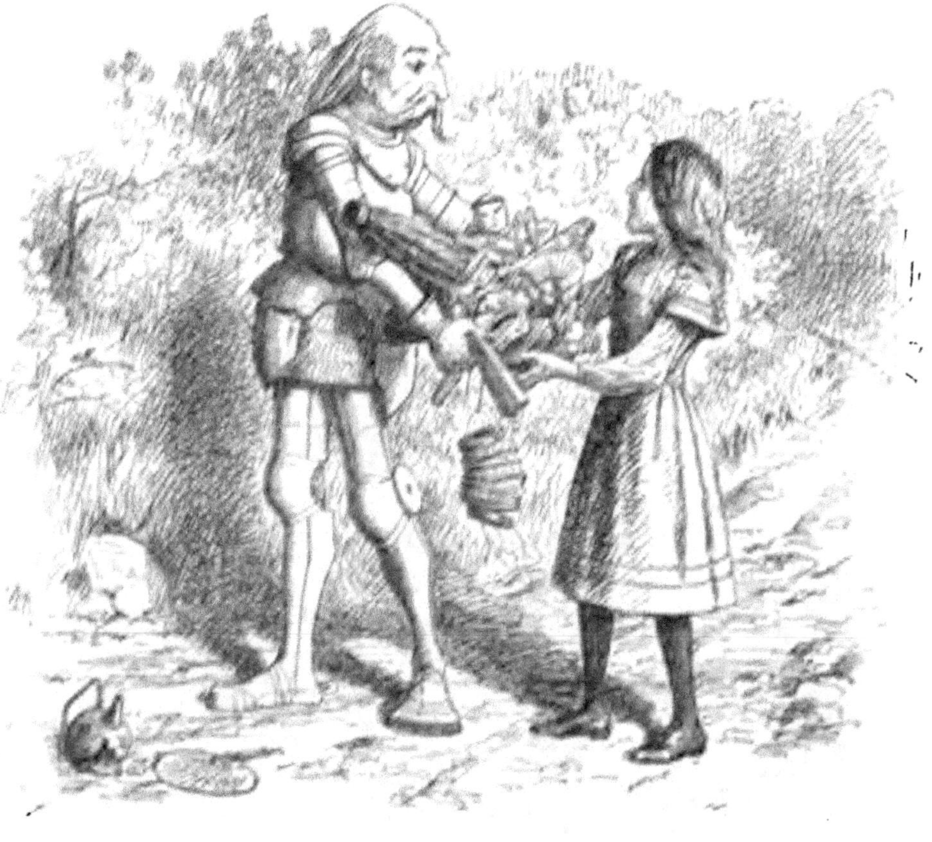

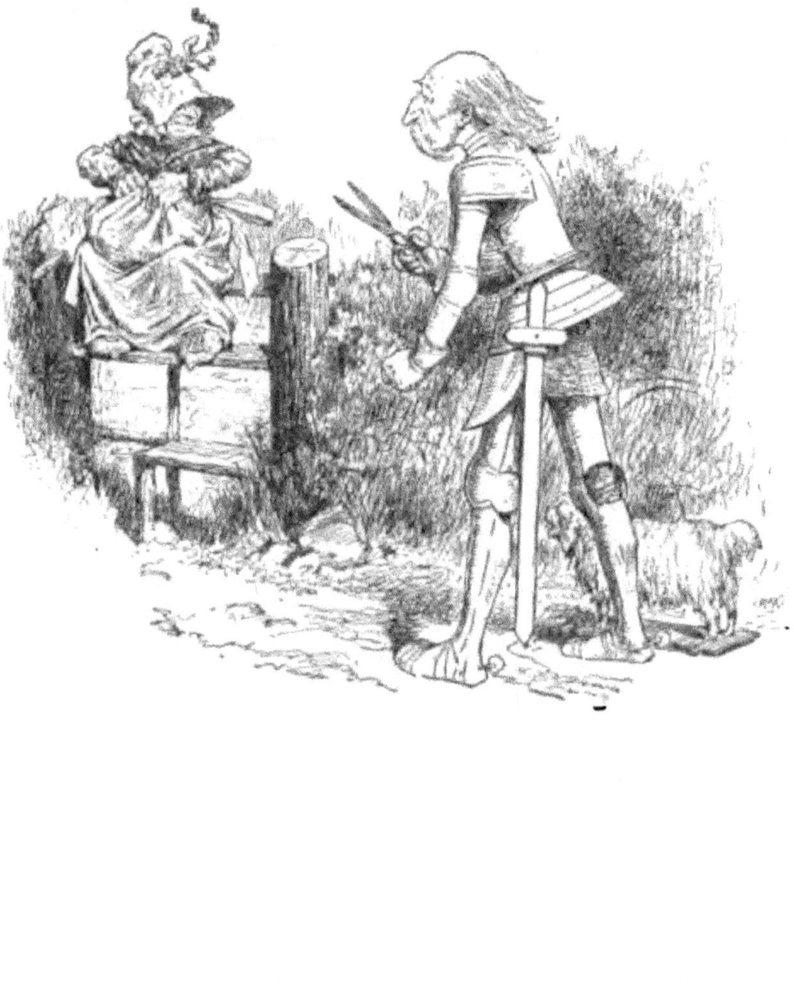

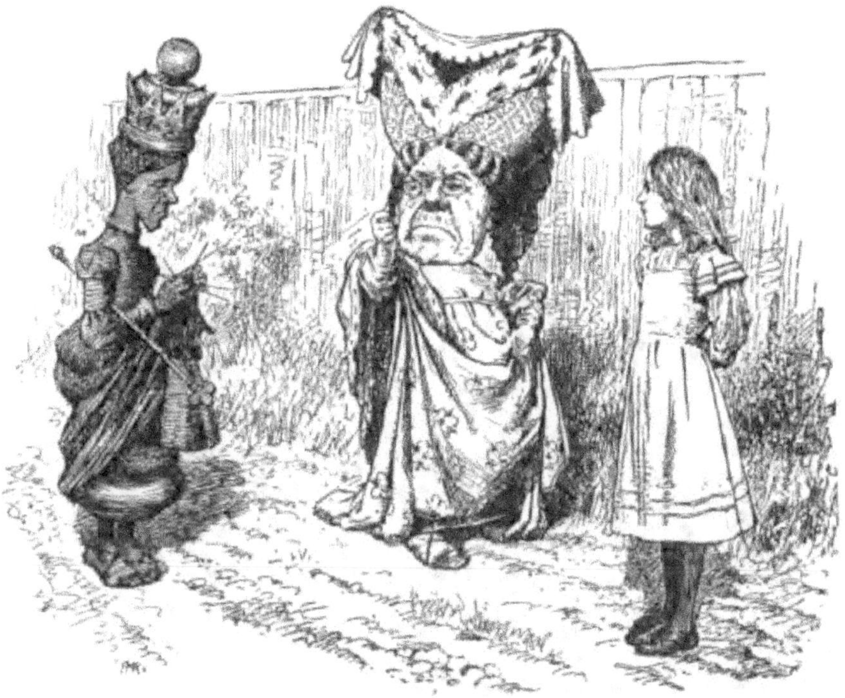

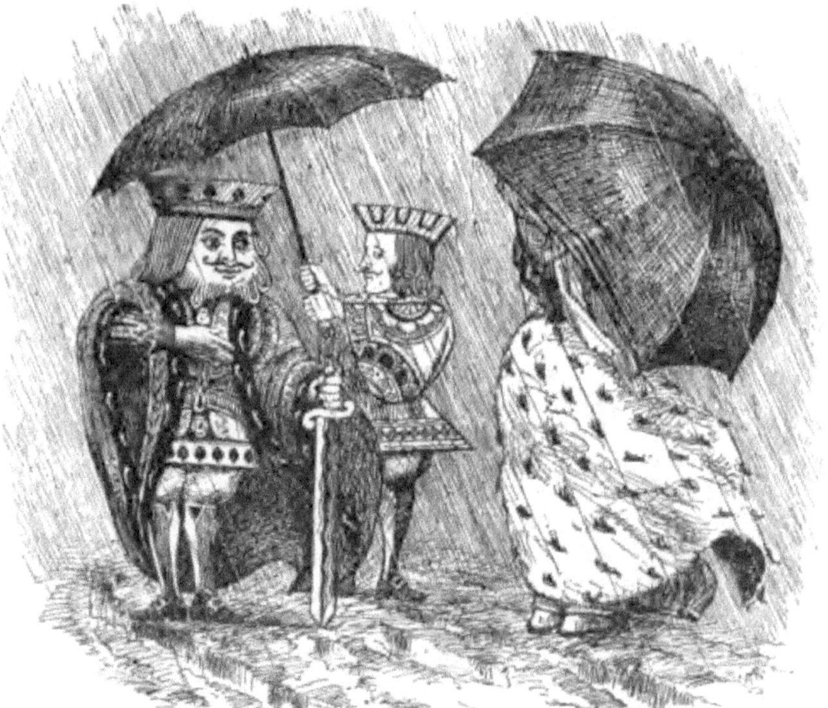

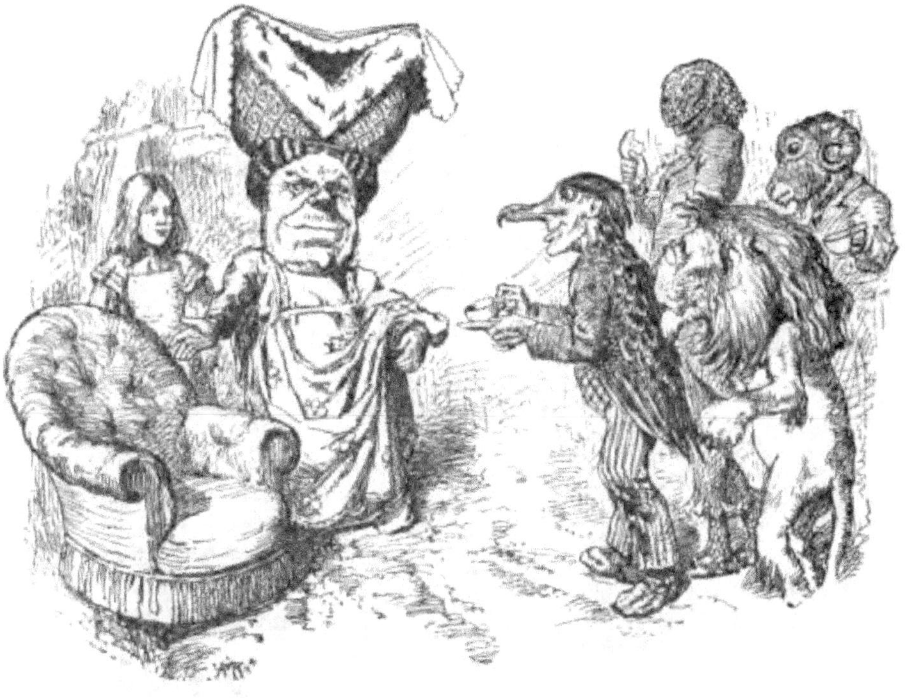

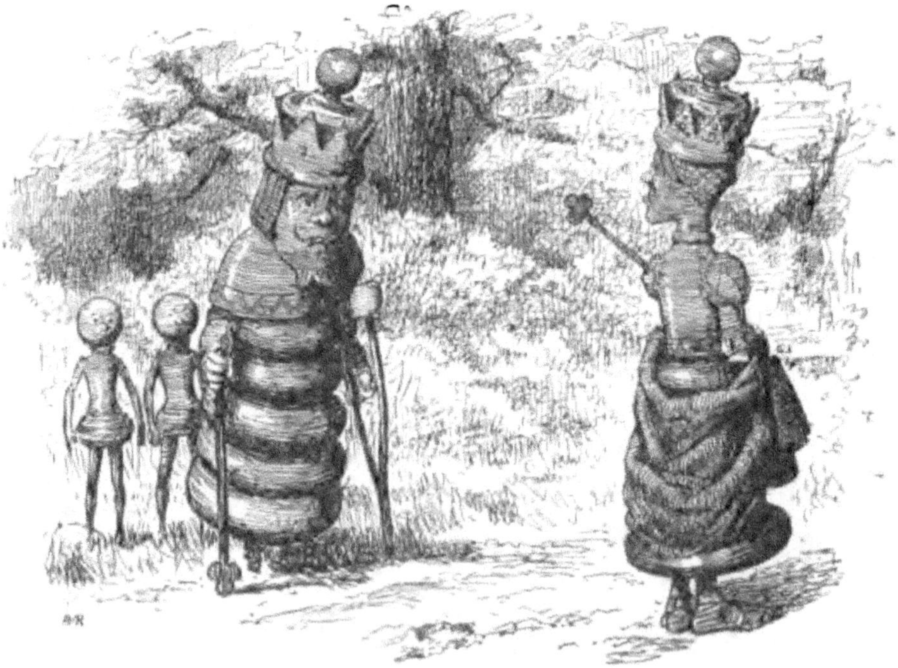

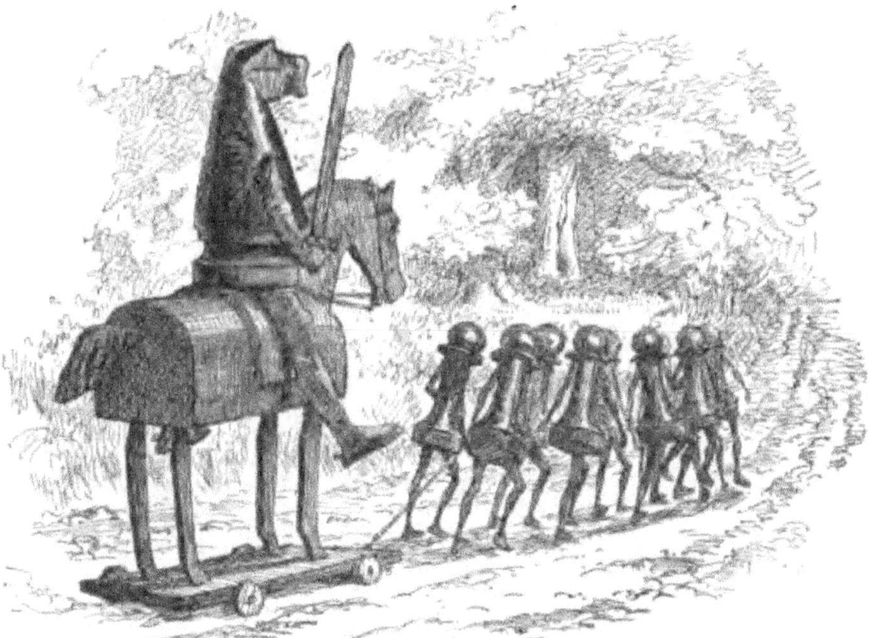

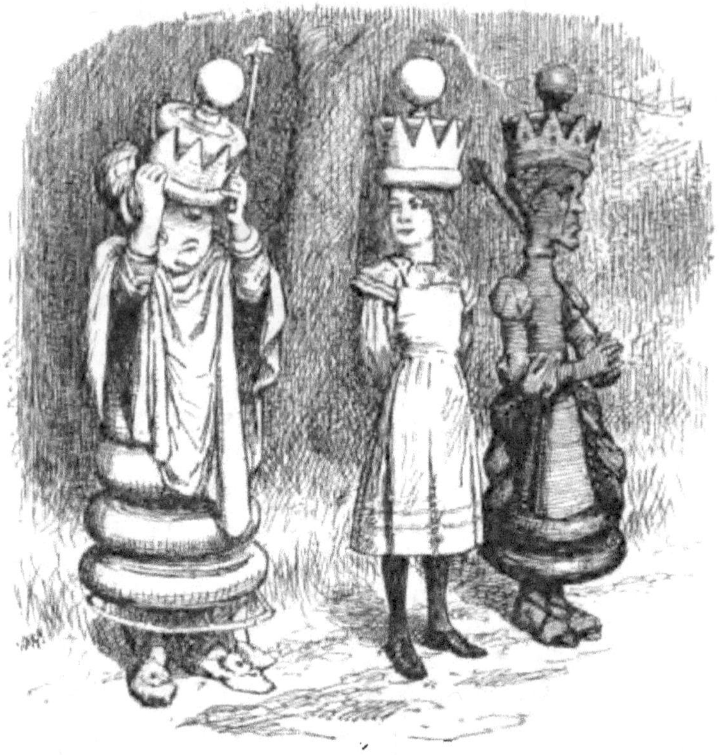

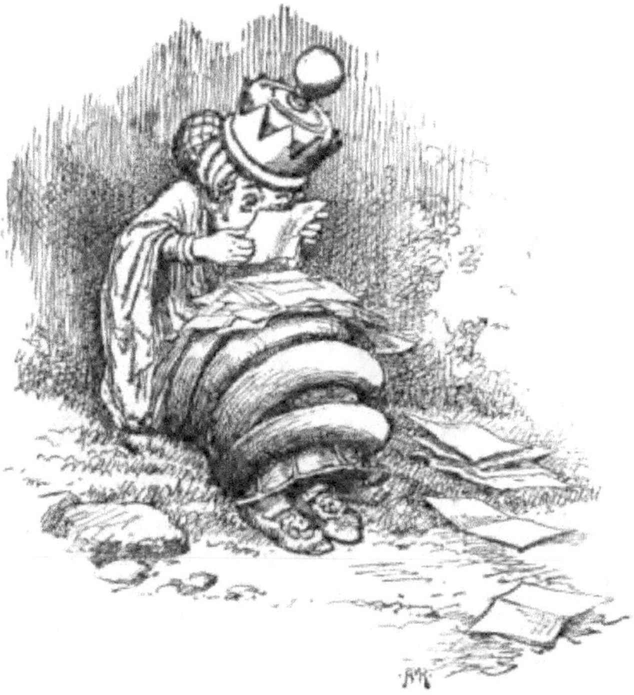

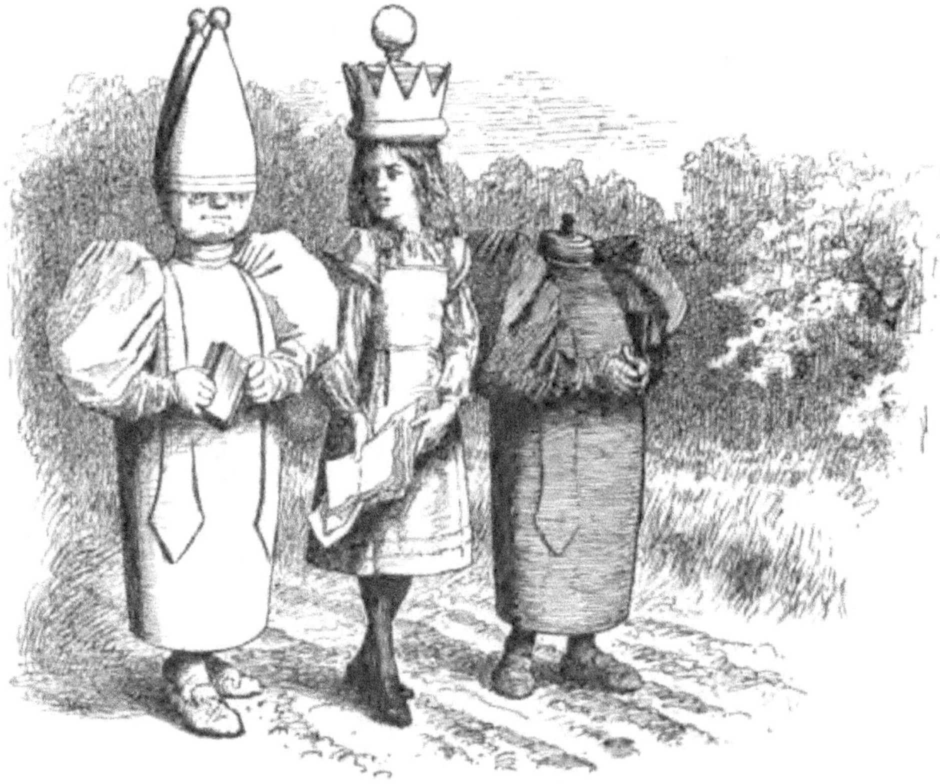

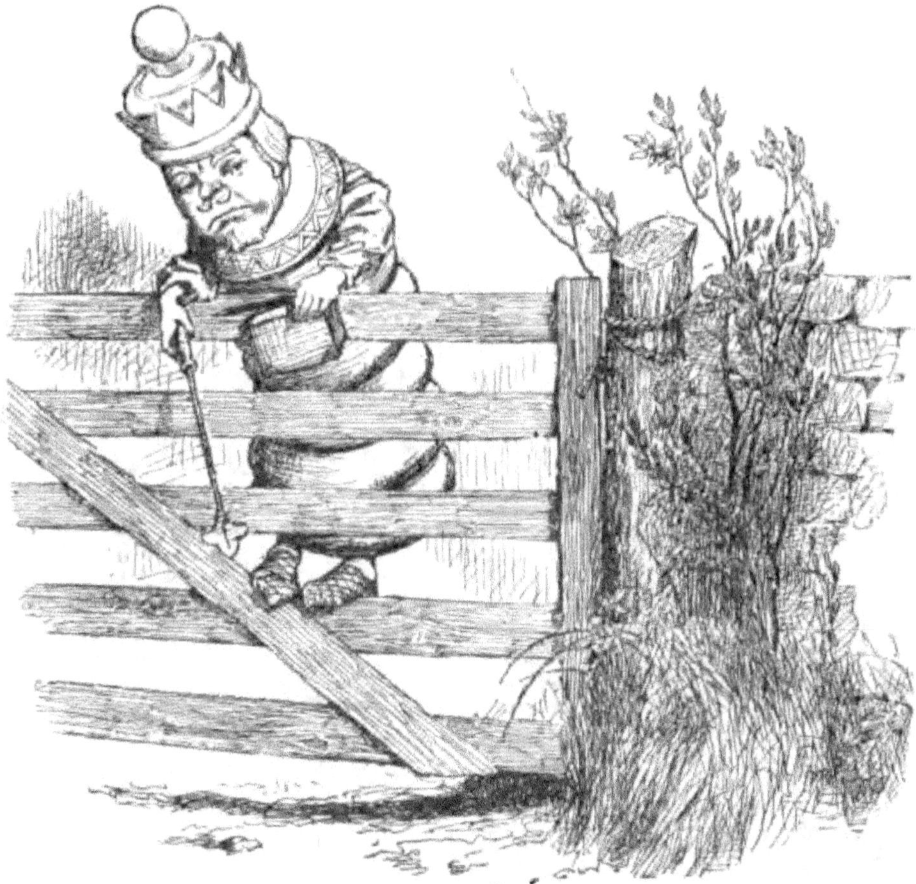

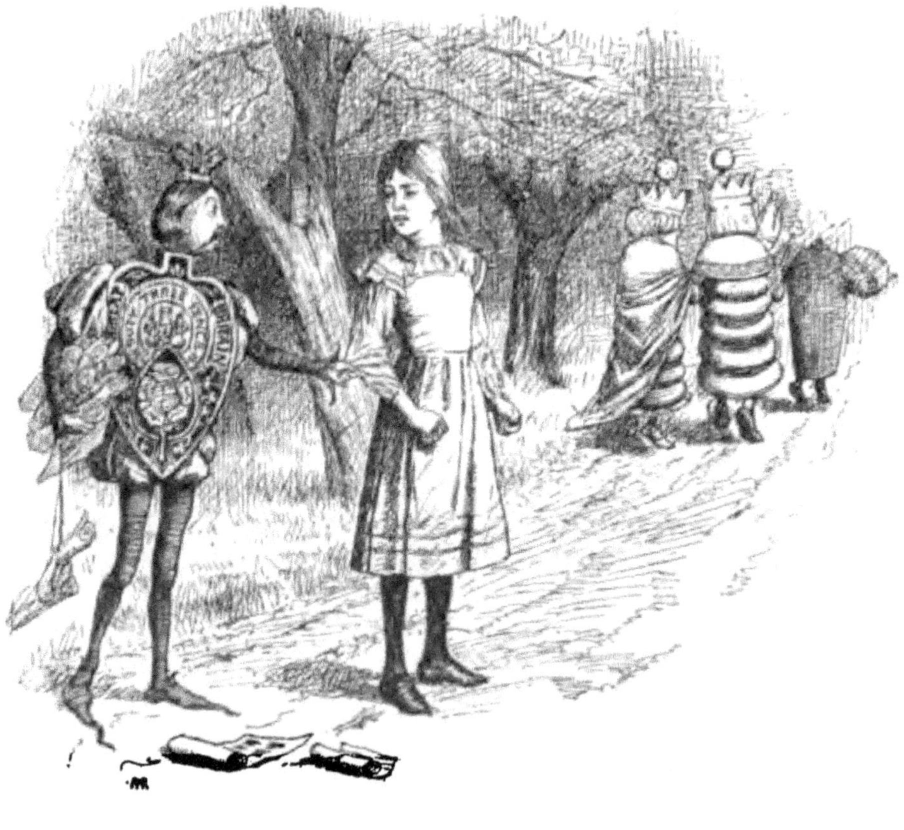

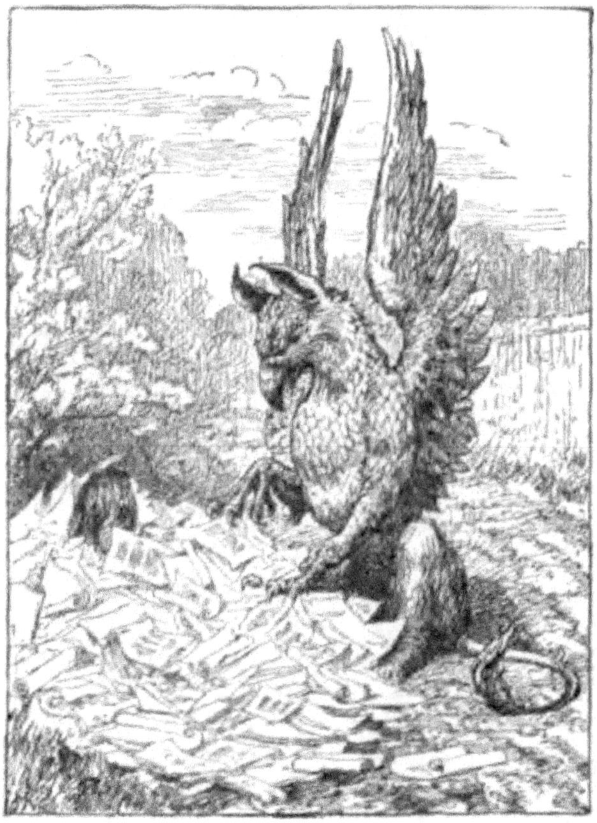

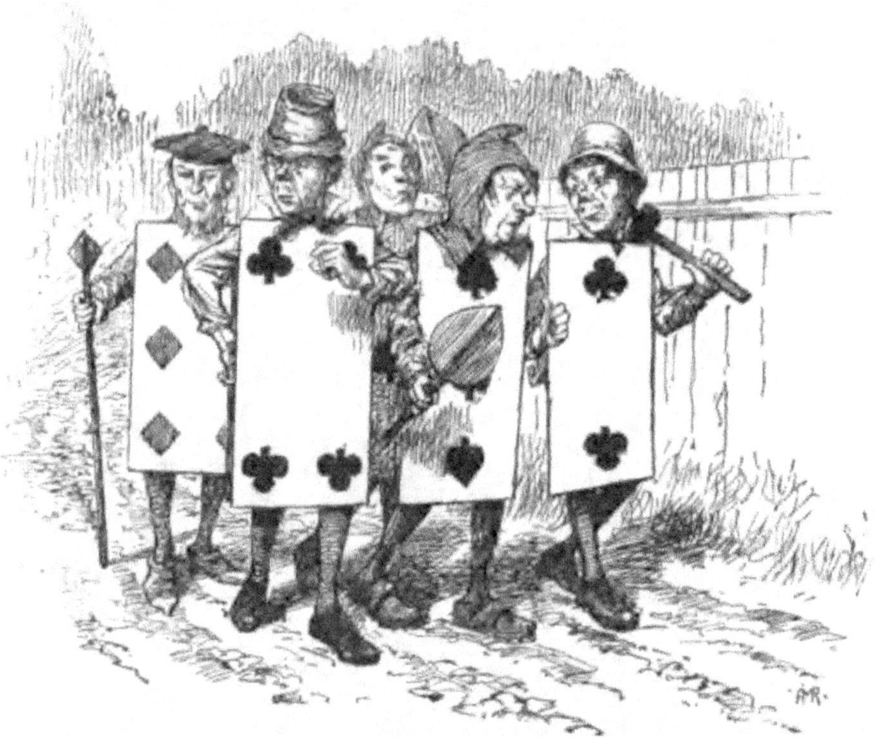

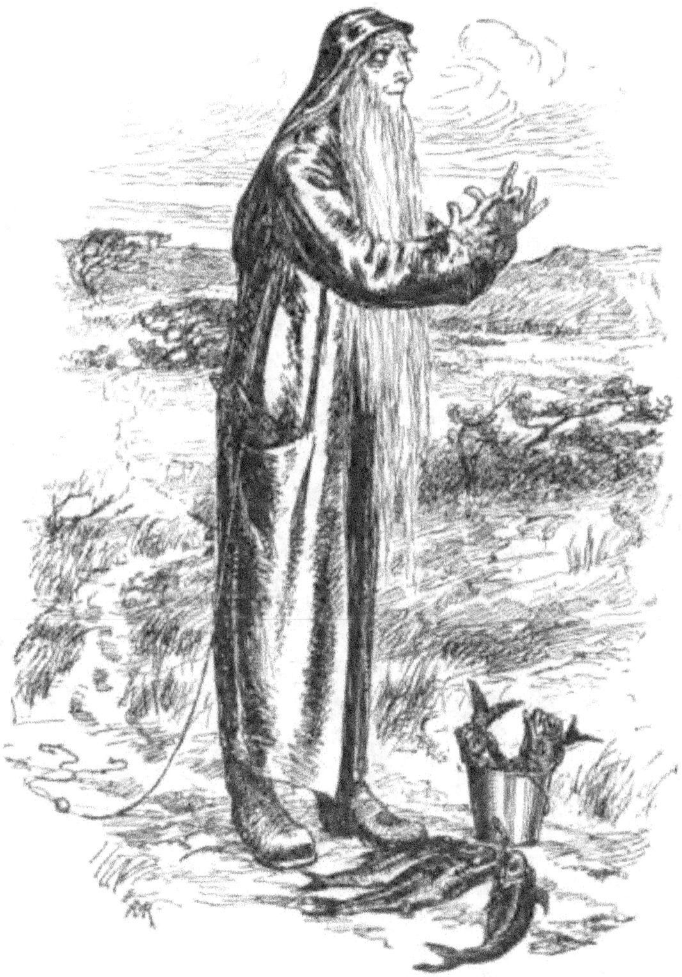

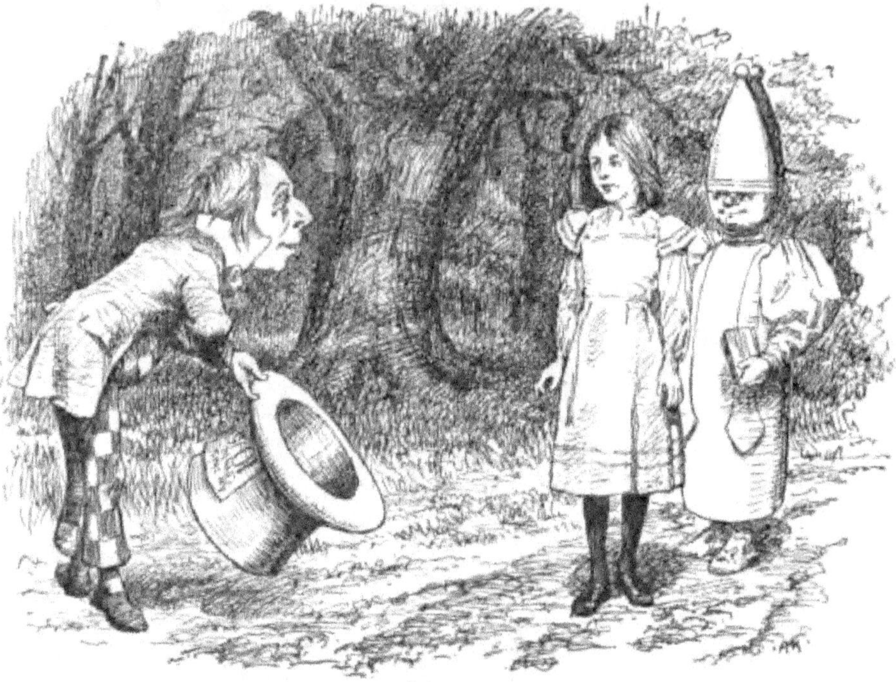

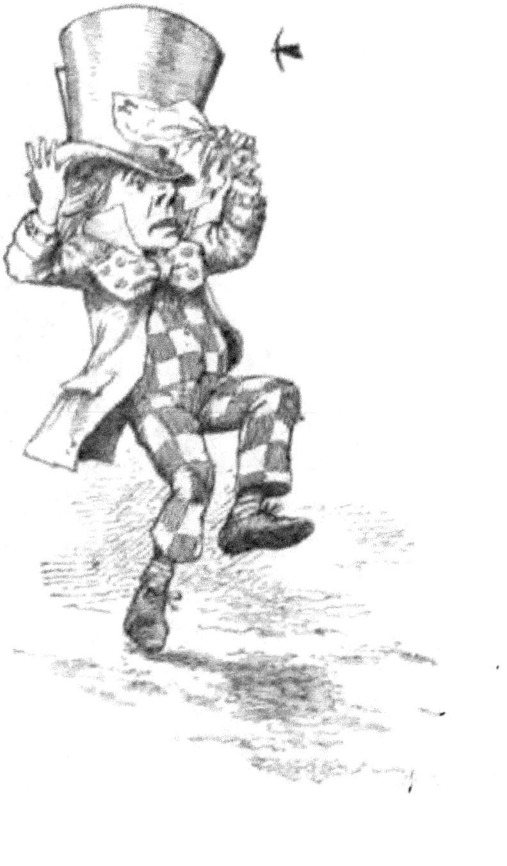

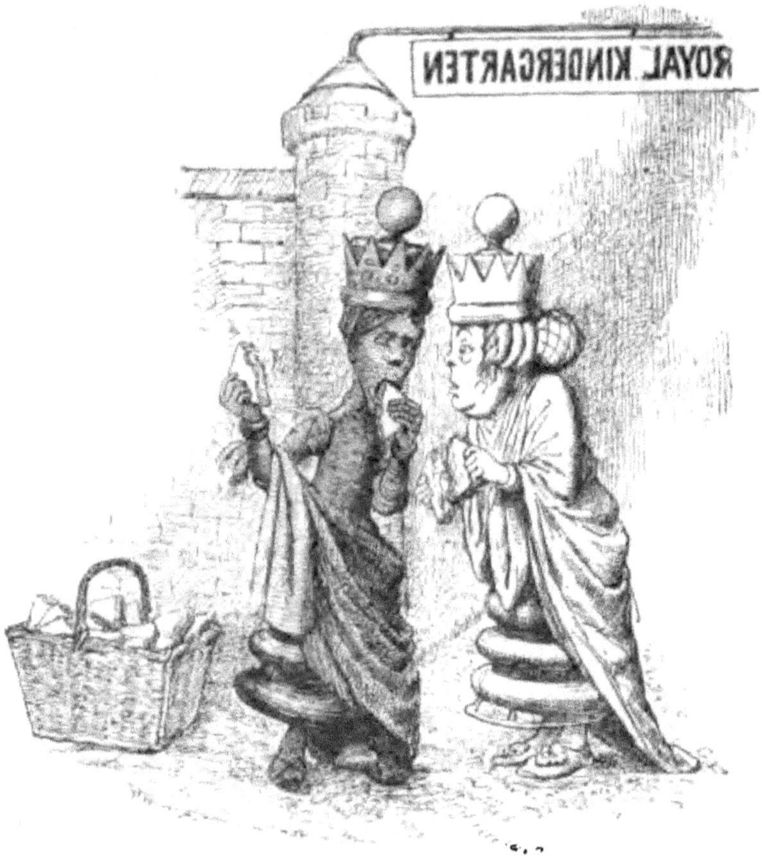
ROYAL KINDERGARTEN

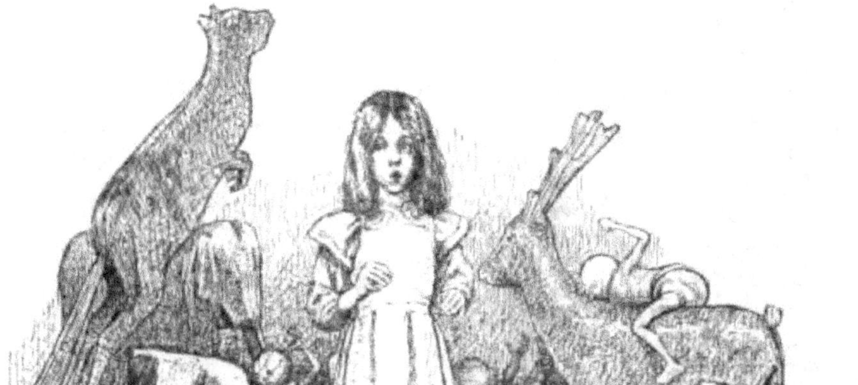

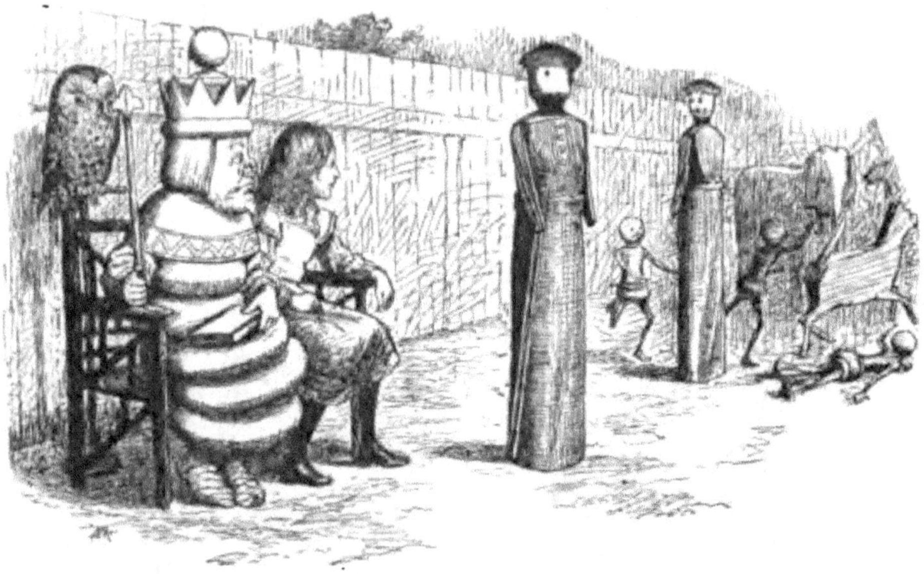

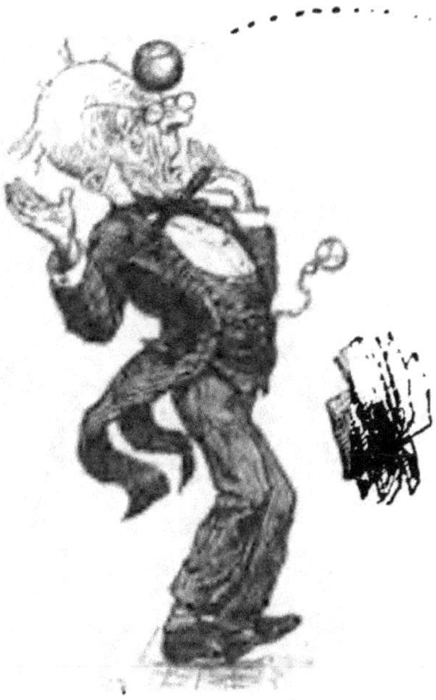

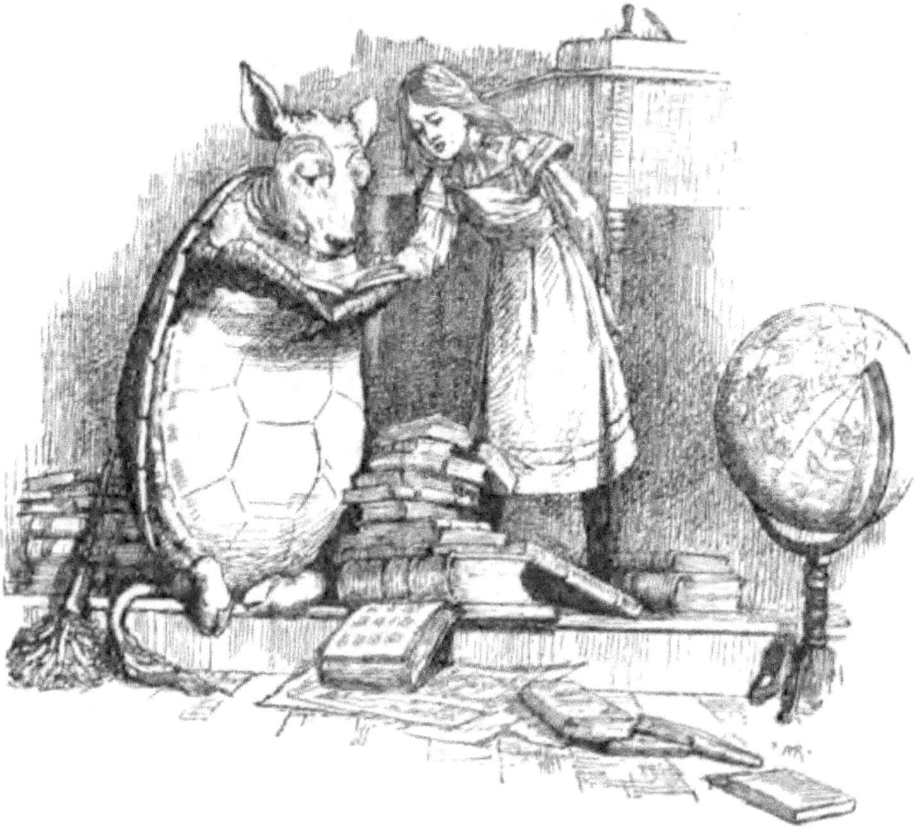

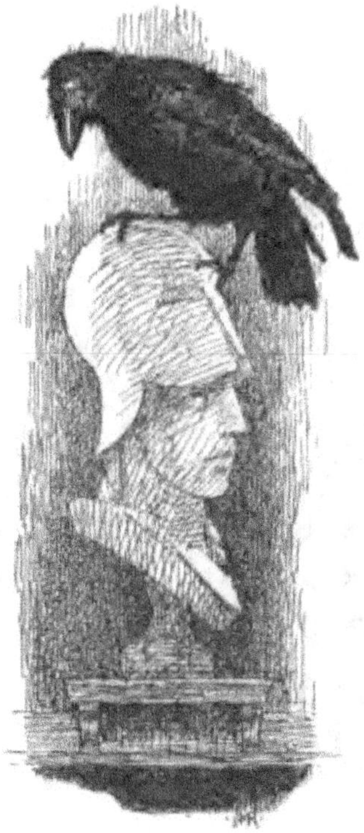

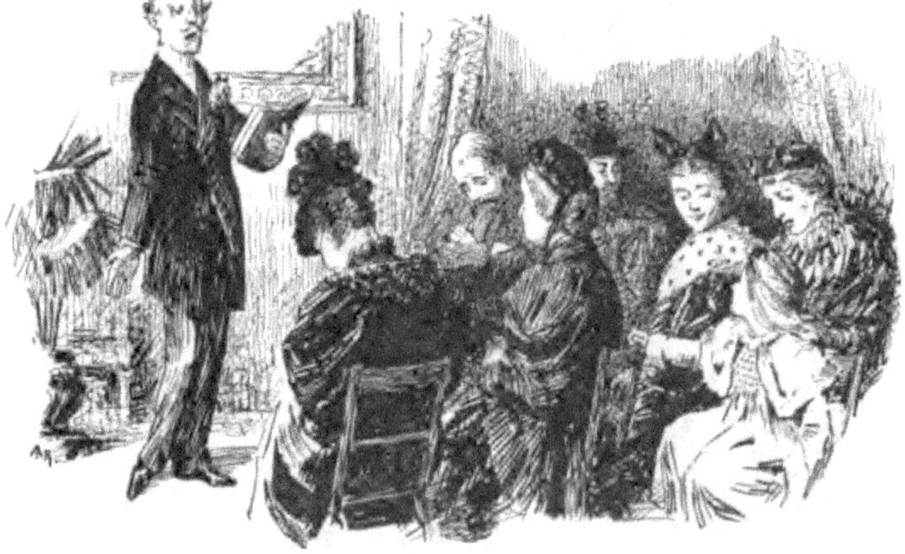

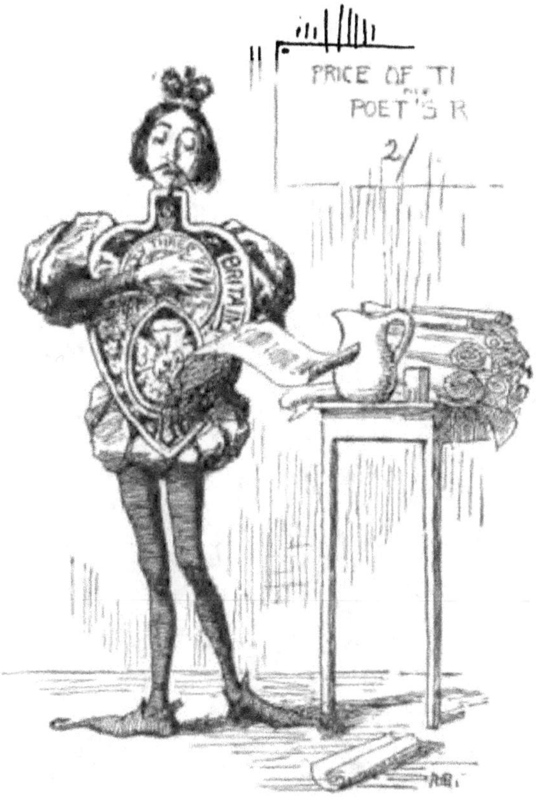
PRICE OF TI
POET'S R
2/
BRITAIN

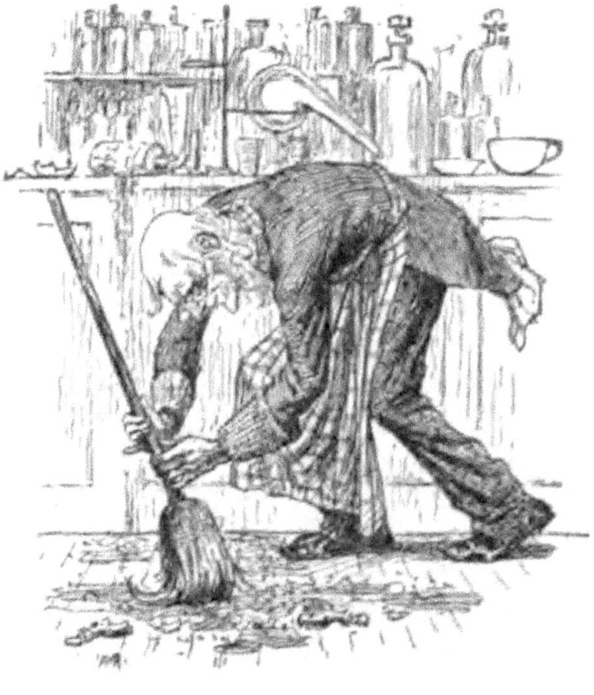

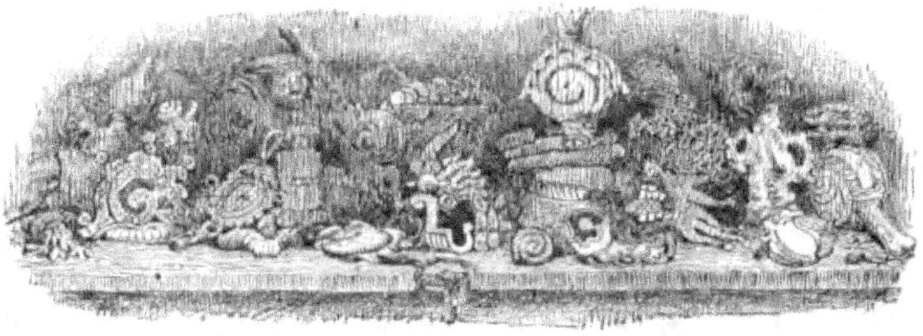

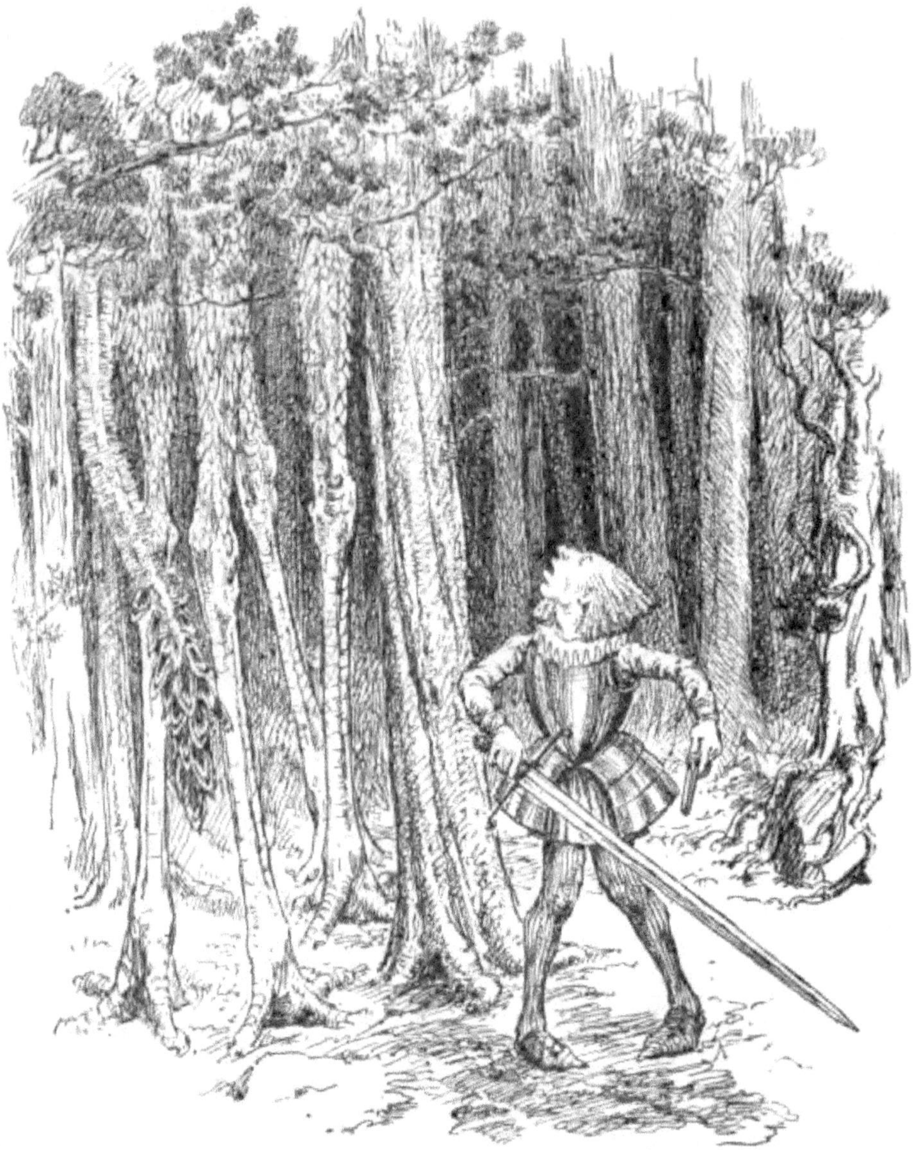

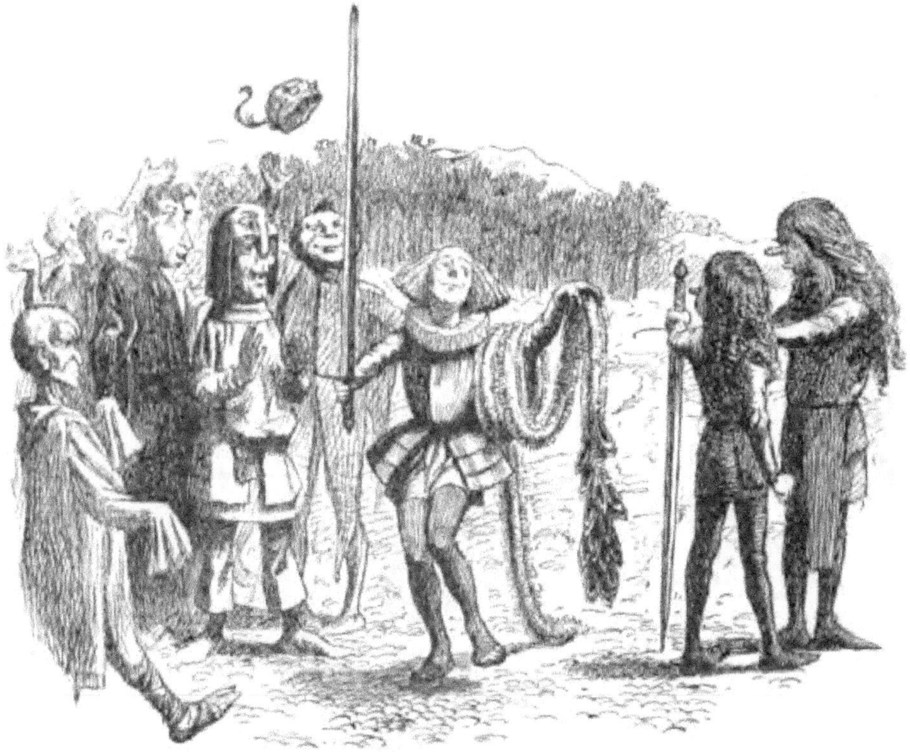

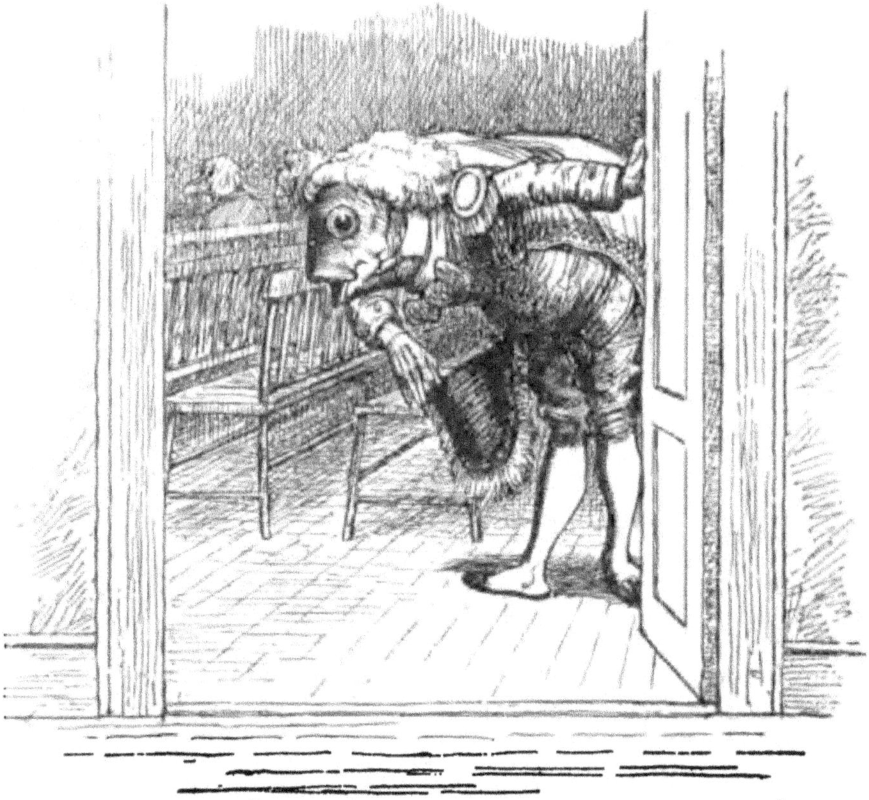

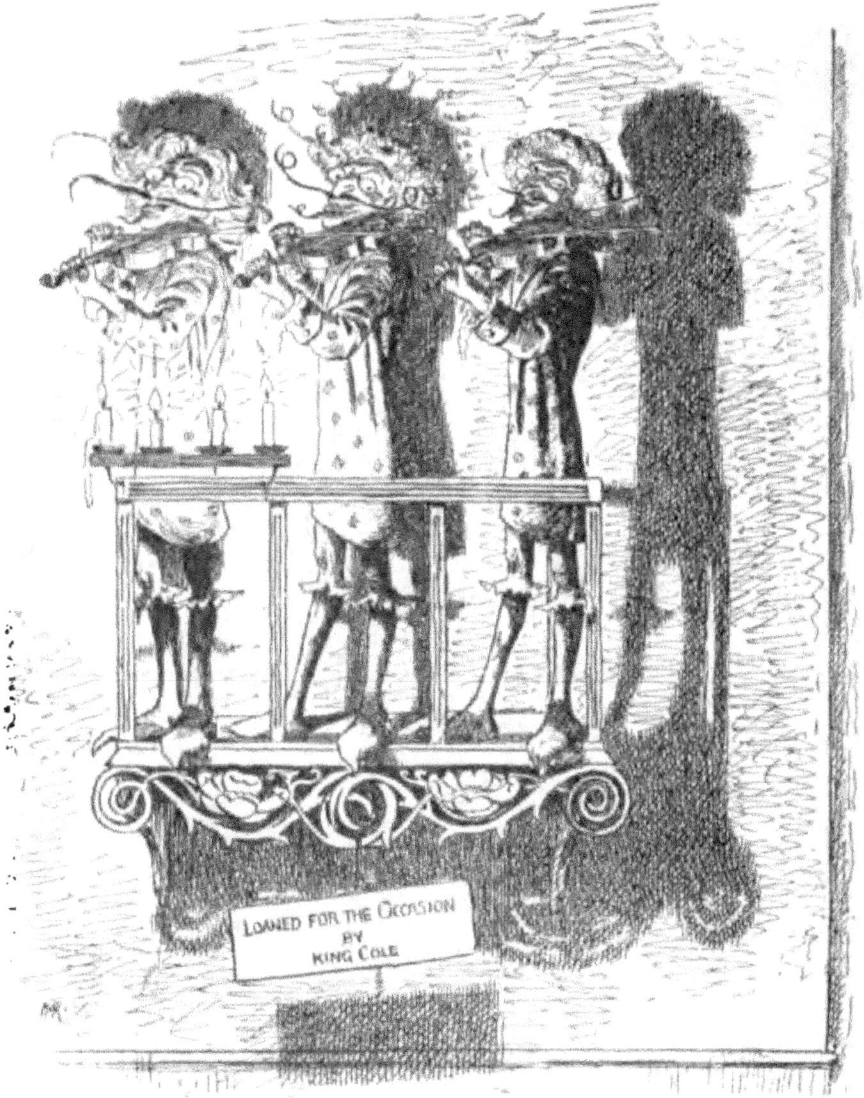
LOANED FOR THE OCCASION
BY
KING COLE

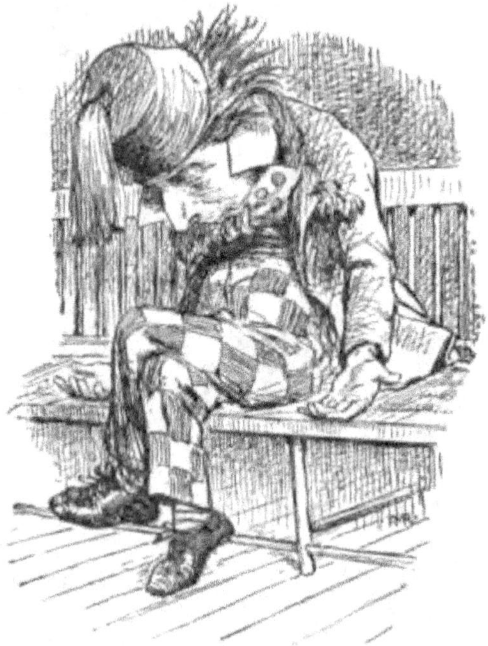

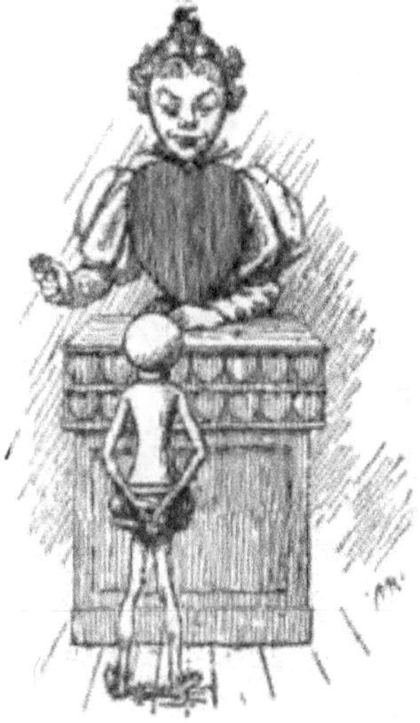

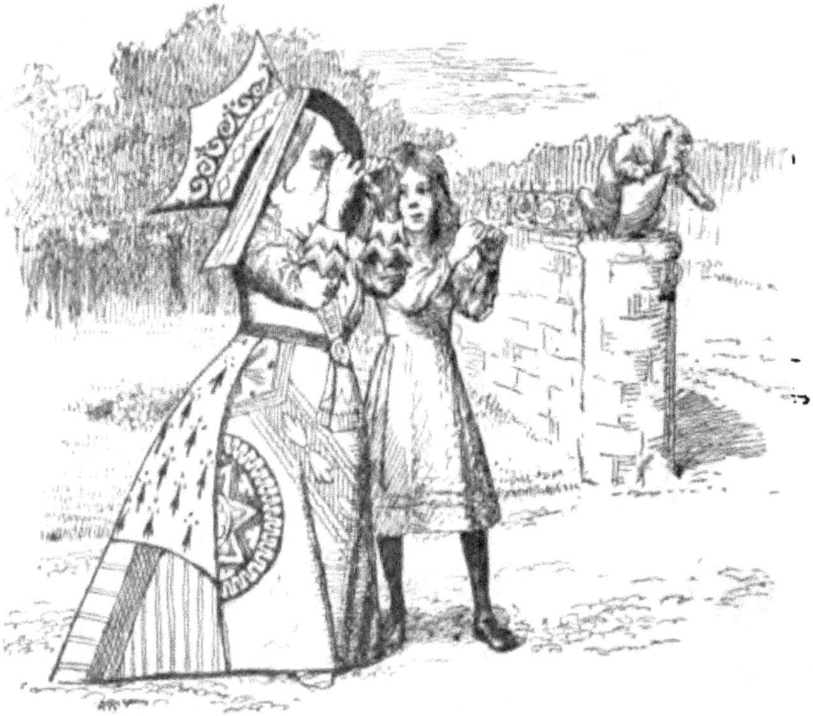

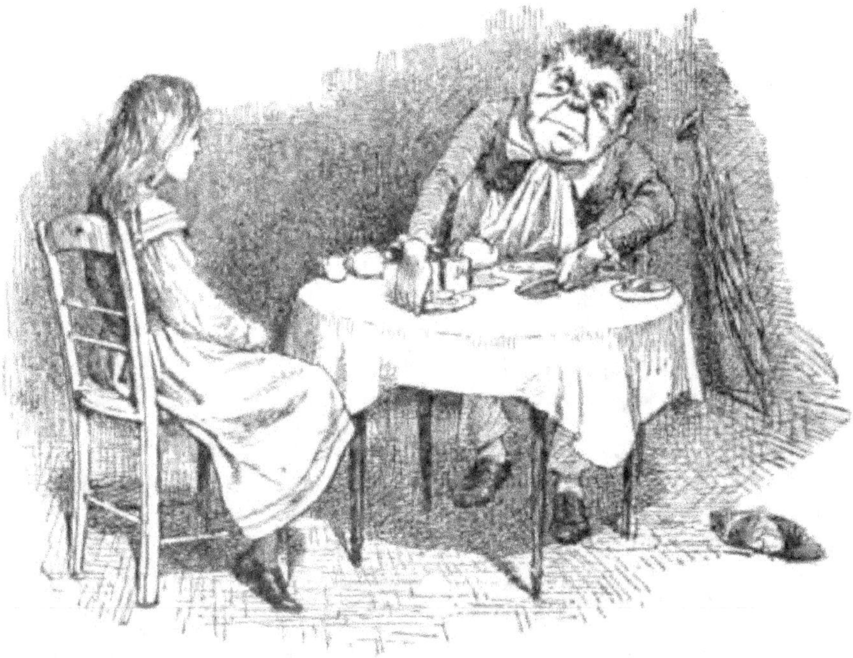

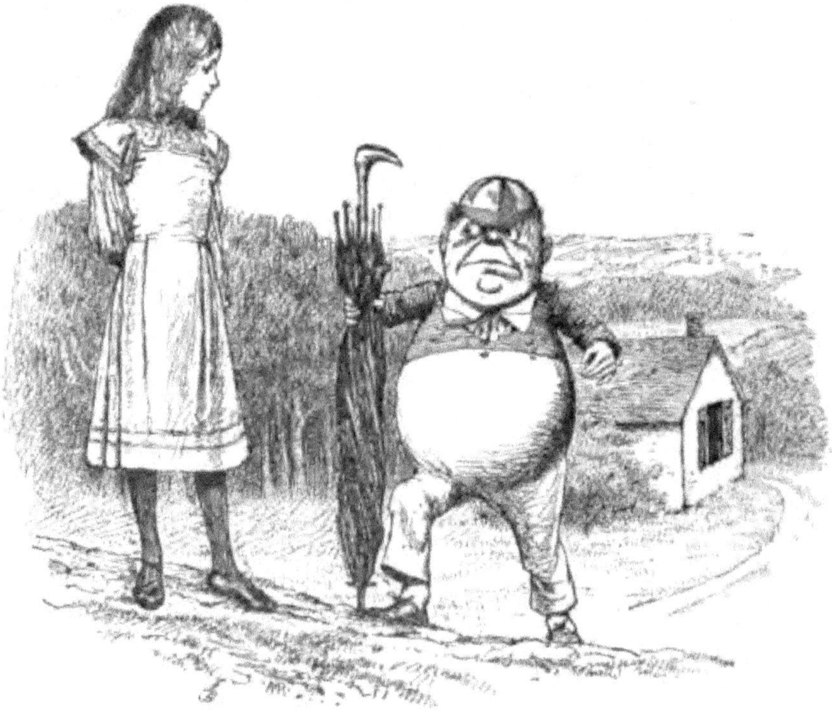

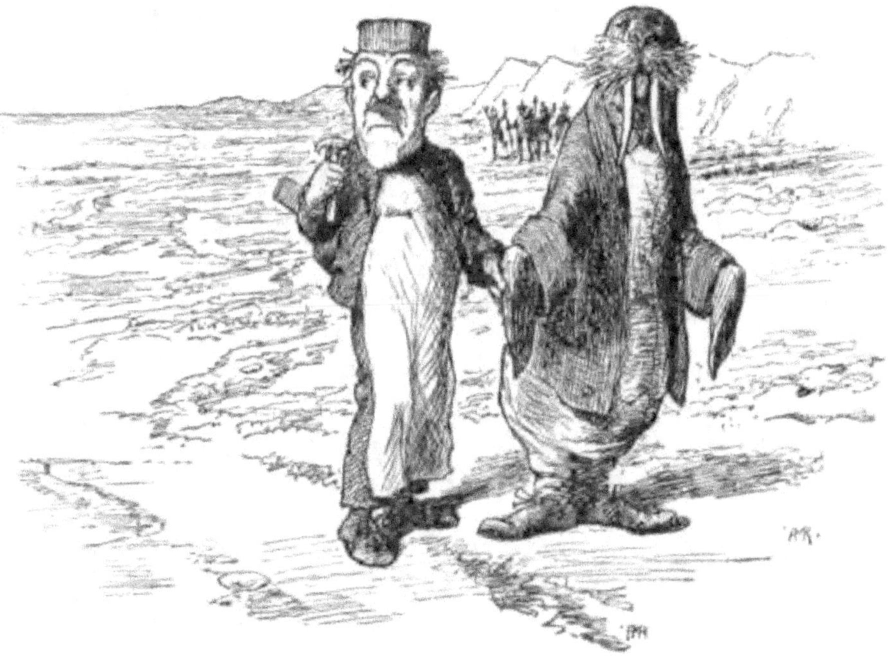

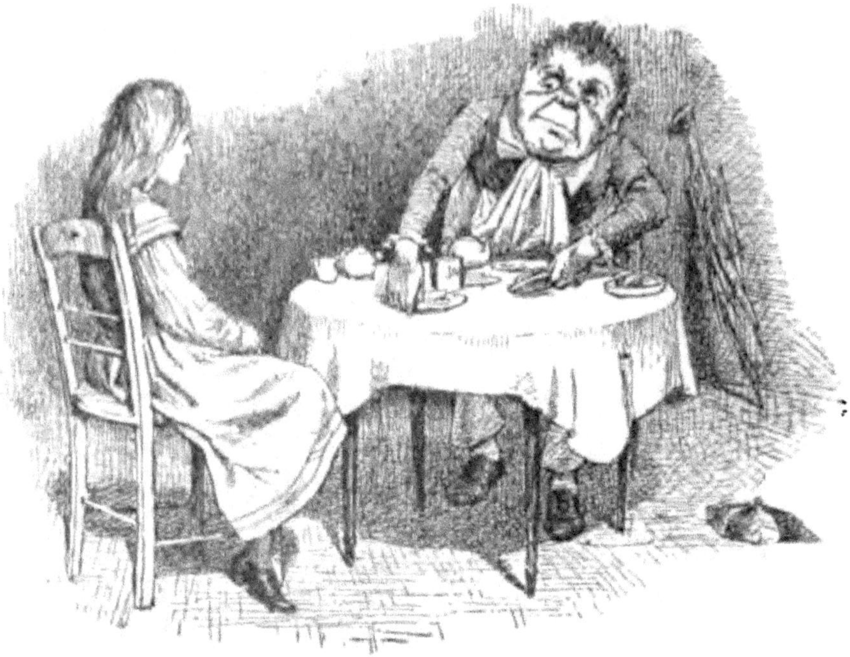

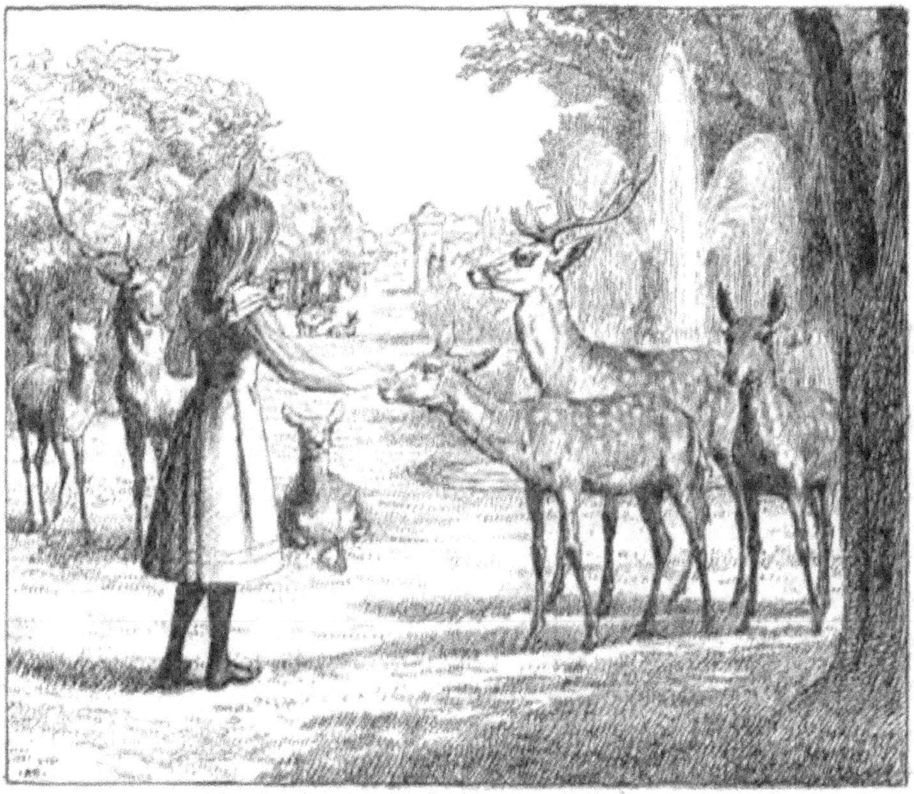

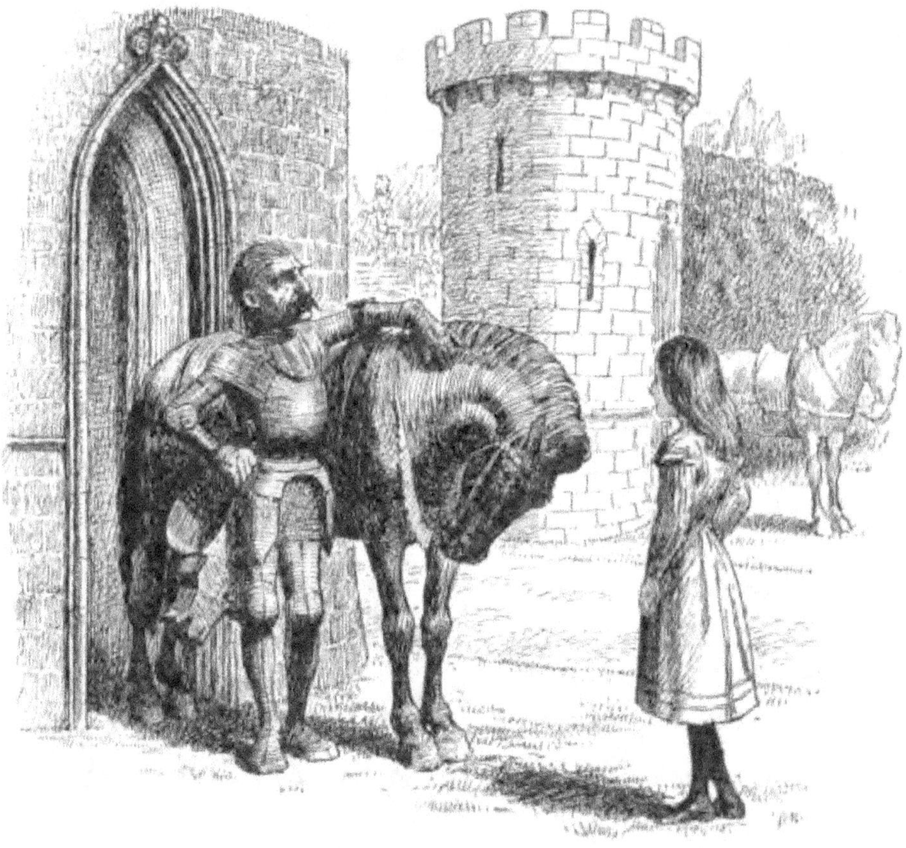

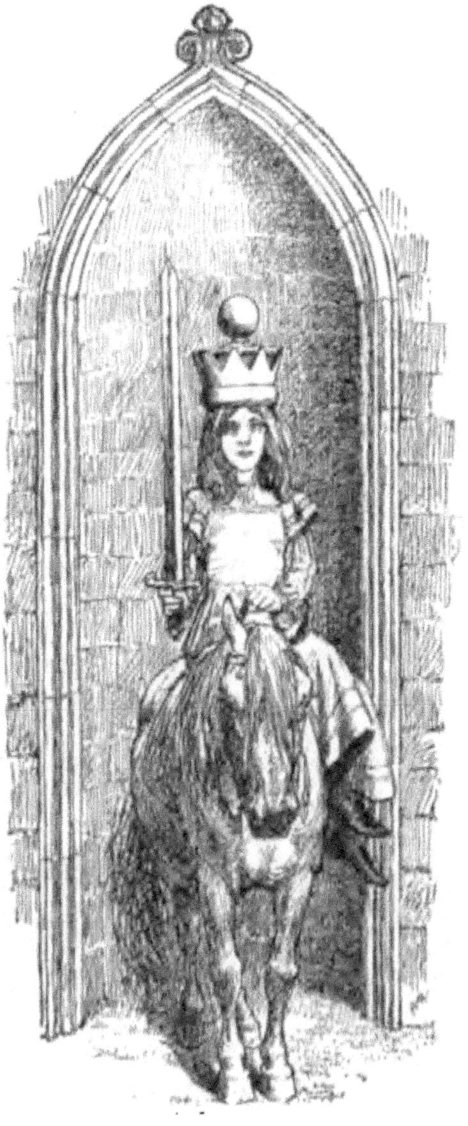

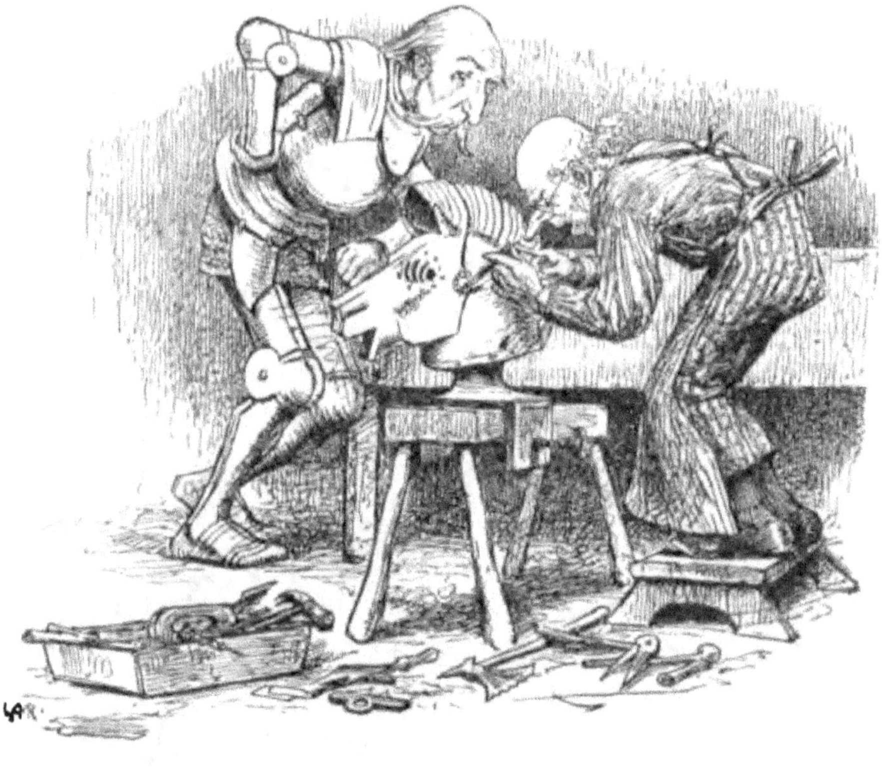

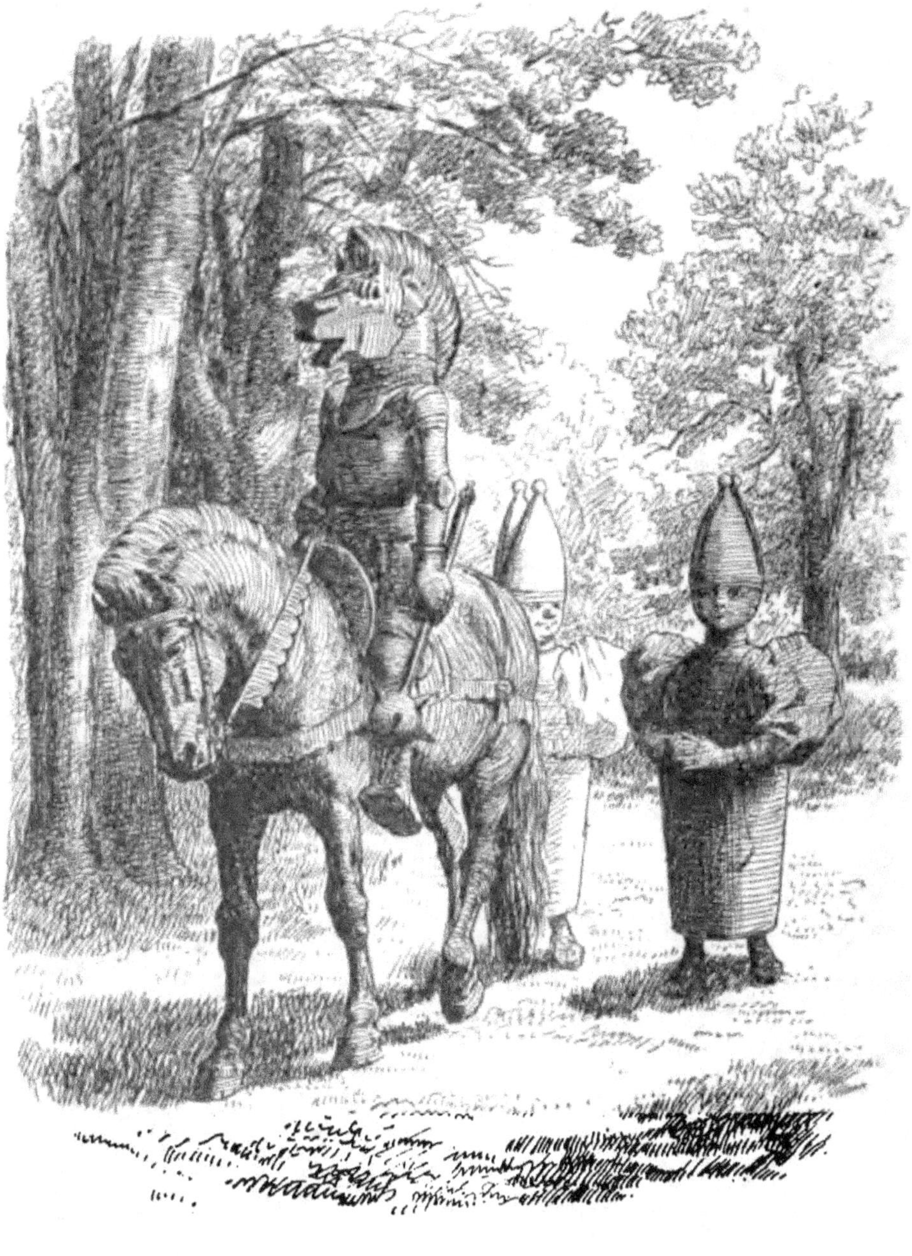

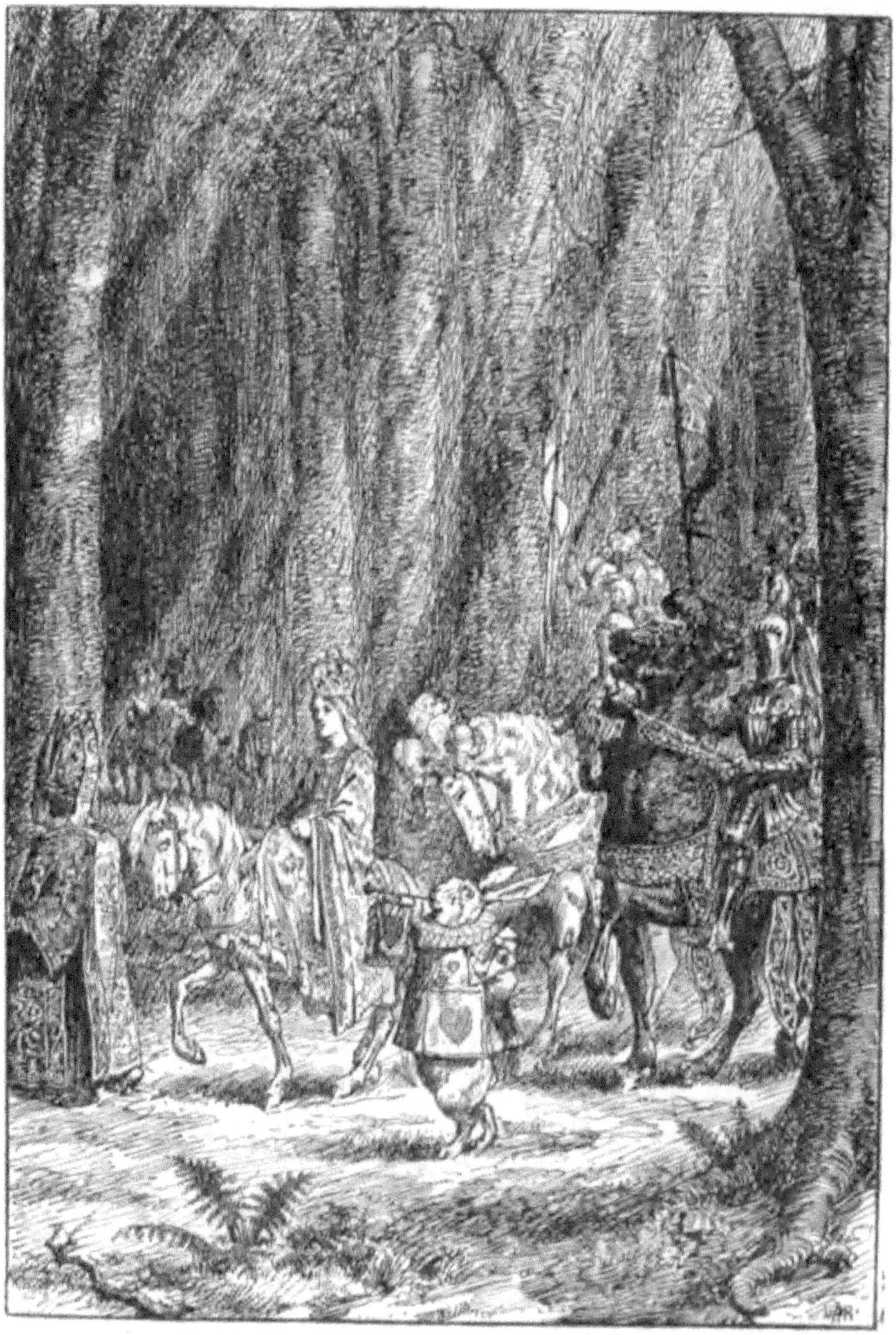

www.ingramcontent.com/pod-product-compliance
Lightning Source LLC
Chambersburg PA
CBHW082218220526
45470CB00010B/3219